Recipes for Elegant but Simple Dining

EVELYN PATTERSON

author of Meals for Guests
Gourmet Kitchen

RECIPES FOR SIMPLE

ELEGANT BUT DINING

COLLIER BOOKS, New York, N.Y.

Collier–Macmillan Ltd., London

A Collier Books Original

Published simultaneously by
Collier-Macmillan Limited, London

First Edition 1963

Collier Books is a division of The Crowell-Collier
Publishing Company

Contents

Recipes for Elegant but Simple Dining

THE BEGINNING

Fashions in dining may not be as erratic as fashions in dressing. But they do have trends. Perhaps it would be more accurate to say that food fashions are like clothing fashions: they go in circles. For those who care about food, the days of the quite informal dinner are now past. We have come almost full circle, back to the well-set table with more than one course. In this cookless and maidless country we are not likely to go all the way back to the six- to eight-course dinner. But the three- to four-course dinner, informally served, is with us again.

The "what" for the first course is very important, for at the beginning of a meal the edge on the appetite is sharp and the taste buds very keen. The entire meal will be better received if it is gotten off to a good start; and if the diners are put into the proper mood, they will savor the second course more leisurely and appreciatively.

The first course must be chosen not merely because of its own virtues, but also in relation to the rest of the meal. Let your main course determine whether your first course is a soup, a pasta, a quiche, a coquille, or a fruit.

Many first courses can play a double role in your cooking repertoire. In slightly larger portions, for example, they may be served as the main dish at lunch or supper. Or vice versa: many dishes which you have always thought of as main-course dishes may be served, in slightly smaller portions, as a first course. This is not true of roasts, steaks, or chops, of course, but is true of most fish dishes and pasta dishes as well as sweetbreads, kidneys, chicken livers, and various casserole combinations.

All the recipes yield six servings.

Soups

I HAVE OFTEN HEARD and read that soup-making is the greatest art in cooking. This statement is, I think, an exaggeration. Anyone who can read and follow directions and is willing to spend a little extra time can make good soups.

The stock, or basis of the soup, is the most important element in soup-making. If the stock is good, it is relatively easy to make a tasty soup, but if the stock is watery or off-flavor, it is impossible. However, to make a good stock is not at all difficult. If the right—and the freshest —ingredients are used and a little care is taken in the preparation, anyone can make a good stock, and from the stock a good soup. On first reading, the directions may perhaps sound tedious and time consuming, but that impression would be erroneous: because a stock may have to simmer for hours, you do not have to watch it all the time; moreover, stock can be made in large quantities and stored in the refrigerator for days, or it can be frozen for future use. Any large pot of stock will thus provide the basis for many delicious soups and sauces.

All soup recipes can be fitted into four main categories: 1) thin clear soups, such as consommé, bouillon, and broth;

11

2) light delicate cream soups and bisques; 3) heavy thick soups, such as chowders, minestrone, vegetable soup, and thick hearty cream soups, usually meals in themselves; 4) chilled or jellied soups, usually served in the summer.

There are four basic stocks which can be made at home very efficiently, and these will cover all the soups that a housewife will want to make. White stock is used for most light cream soups. Brown stock is used for clear strong consommés, for hearty vegetable soups, and, when reduced, for meat glazes and for brown sauces. Chicken stock is used for many cream soups and for sauces to be served with poultry and for poaching chickens or quenelles. Fish stock is used for seafood and fish bisques and soups, and for sauces to be served with seafood and fish.

WHITE STOCK (4 QUARTS)

3 *pounds neck and shin of beef, cracked*
2 *pounds lean beef*
1½ *pounds necks, wings, and backs of chicken*
6 *quarts cold water*
1 *tablespoon salt*
1 *pound carrots, scraped and cut into 1-inch hunks*

1 *large turnip, quartered*
1 *large parsnip, quartered (optional)*
4 *leeks (if not available, use an extra onion)*
2 *stalks celery*
1 *large onion with 2 whole cloves stuck into it*

Put the meat and bones into a large kettle. Add the chicken parts, water, and salt. Place the pot on a low fire so that it will come to a boil slowly. Stir the pot occasionally during this stage and remove the scum as it rises to the top. The clearness of the stock depends on this skimming process. When the pot begins to simmer, add the vegetables. Again remove the scum as it rises and wipe the edge of the pot clean of deposit as it forms. After simmering and skimming for 10 minutes, cover the pot and continue to simmer very gently for 5 hours. Remove from fire and add 2 cups cold water to help coagulate the grease which will rise to the surface. Carefully remove the grease and then strain the stock, first through a strainer and then through a fine cheesecloth. Cool stock quickly, especially in summer, when fermentation sets in easily.

BROWN STOCK (4 QUARTS)

2 pounds neck and shin of beef, cracked quite fine
1 knuckle of veal, cracked quite fine
1 pound stewing beef, cut into cubes and well browned
6 quarts cold water
1 tablespoon salt
2 carrots, scraped and cut into hunks
2 onions, halved and stuck with 2 whole cloves
1 turnip, quartered
2 stalks celery, cut into large pieces
Bouquet garni (2 bay leaves, thyme, parsley, whole peppercorns tied into a small cheesecloth sack)

Brown the bones in a hot oven. Sear the meat until dark brown in a little butter or margarine in a hot skillet. Put the bones and meat into a large soup kettle, cover with cold water, add salt. Let stand for 1 hour, then put on a low fire and bring slowly to a boil, skimming off the scum as it rises. When quite clear, add the vegetables and bouquet garni. Again bring slowly to a boil, skimming well. Cover and simmer very gently for 5 hours. Do not stir, but skim occasionally. Strain first through a strainer and then through a fine cheesecloth. When cool, remove fat that has coagulated on surface. Store in refrigerator or freezer.

CHICKEN STOCK

This is prepared in exactly the same way as White Stock, substituting 1 old hen or 3 pounds chicken parts and a cracked veal knuckle for the beef bones and meat.

CLARIFIED STOCK FOR CONSOMMÉ

The clarifying process is essential only when you are using your stock for a clear consommé or bouillon. For other soups and for sauces it is unnecessary if your stock has been well-skimmed and thoroughly strained through a fine cheesecloth.

The following procedure of clarification is for all stocks except fish stock.

For each 4 quarts of stock:

1 *small onion, chopped coarsely*

1 *carrot, scraped and cut into 1-inch pieces*

3 *sprigs celery*

Bouquet garni (1 bay leaf, pinch thyme, 2 sprigs tarragon or a pinch of the dry herb, pinch or sprig of chervil, parsley and 1

whole clove) tied together in small piece of cheesecloth

White and shell of 1 egg

1 *teaspoon lemon juice*

1 *tablespoon white wine vinegar*

½ *pound ground lean beef moistened with 2 tablespoons water*

Place all the ingredients in a soup kettle and cover with 4 quarts of stock. Place the kettle on a low heat and bring slowly to the boiling point, stirring with a wire whisk the entire time. Then allow it to simmer gently, uncovered and without stirring for ½ hour. Taste for seasoning. Strain through a fine cheesecloth. Cool and store in the refrigerator unless you are going to use it at once for clear soup or consommé.

FISH STOCK (2 QUARTS)

2 *pounds inexpensive raw white fish, bones and trimmings included*
1½ *tablespoons salt*
3 *onions, sliced*
3 *carrots, sliced*
10 *slightly bruised peppercorns*

Bouquet garni (thyme, parsley, bay leaf, green celery leaves tied together in a small piece of cheesecloth)
5 *cups cold water*
3 *cups dry white wine*

Put all ingredients in a soup kettle, bring slowly to a boil on a low heat, cover and simmer very gently for ½ hour. Do not cook longer or stock will tend to become bitter. Strain twice through fine cheesecloth and use as directed.

CREAM SOUPS DU JOUR

Given a good white stock, 1 onion for piquancy, and 2 medium potatoes for thickening for every pint of stock, you can be as imaginative as you like and make many varieties of delicious soups—as many varieties as there are suitable vegetables. Cook the vegetables in the stock until tender, usually about 25 minutes, then put into a blender or through a food mill until well-puréed and smooth. If you do not have a blender or mill, rub through a fine sieve. Now add light cream until you have the consistency you want. Taste for seasoning, reheat, and serve. Voilà!—a perfect start for any meal.

Following are some suggestions for the Cream Soup of the Day.

CARROT CREAM SOUP

1 *quart White Stock (see recipe)*
4 *potatoes, sliced thin*
2 *onions, sliced thin*
8 *carrots, scraped and sliced thin*

2 *stalks celery, finely chopped*
Light cream for thinning, about 2 cups

Cook the vegetables in the stock until tender (about 25 minutes), purée well in a blender or rub through a fine sieve, dilute with the light cream to the consistency desired. Reheat and serve.

CAULIFLOWER CREAM SOUP

1 *quart White Stock (see recipe)*
4 *potatoes, sliced thin*
2 *onions, sliced thin*

½ *medium-sized cauliflower, broken into florets*
1 *teaspoon chervil*
Light cream for thinning, about 2 cups

Simmer the vegetables and chervil in the stock until tender—about 25 minutes. Put into a blender and run until thick and smooth. If you have no blender, rub through a fine sieve. Dilute with the cream to the consistency desired. Check the seasoning. Reheat and serve.

ZUCCHINI CREAM SOUP

Substitute 8 to 10 small zucchini for the carrots or cauliflower, and proceed as directed for those soups in preceding recipes.

MIXED VEGETABLE CREAM SOUP

1 *quart White Stock (see recipe)*
4 *potatoes*
2 *onions*
2 *leeks*
1 *carrot*
½ *cup green beans*

1 *zucchini*
1 *teaspoon chervil*
1 *large stalk celery*
⅓ *cup peas or broccoli*
Light cream for thinning, about 2 cups
Salt and pepper

After cleaning the vegetables, chop them coarsely and put into a soup kettle with the stock. The vegetables may be varied according to what you have on hand. Simmer until tender—about 25 minutes. Put into the blender and run until thick and smooth, or rub through a fine sieve. Dilute with the light cream to the consistency desired. Taste for seasoning. Reheat and serve.

All these soups are better if made at least a day ahead of time. They mellow and become smoother in taste while being stored in the refrigerator. If you wish to keep them for more than two or three days, put into the freezer.

SOUP FAVORITE

6 *large leeks, white part only, sliced thin*
2 *cups sliced mushrooms*
4 *tablespoons butter*
4 *cups Chicken Stock (see recipe)*
Bouquet garni (1 bay leaf, 4 sprigs parsley, pinch thyme tied together in a

small square of cheese-cloth)
4 *potatoes, peeled and sliced thin*
Salt and pepper
2 *egg yolks*
1 *cup light cream*
½ *cup chopped chives for garnish*

Sauté the white part of the leeks, thinly sliced, and the sliced mushrooms in the butter for 5 minutes, stirring constantly. Put into a kettle with the chicken stock, bouquet garni, sliced potatoes, and seasoning. Simmer, covered, for ½ hour. Pour the soup, half at a time, into the blender and run until smooth. Or rub through a fine sieve. Combine the egg yolks with the cream and gradually add it to the hot puréed soup. Heat through, but do not allow it to boil. Garnish each serving with chopped chives.

CREAM OF BARLEY

½ pound coarse pearl barley
1 quart White Stock (see recipe)
1 stalk white celery, cut into pieces
1 large leek, white part only, cut into slices, or 1 medium onion, sliced
Light cream for thinning to desired consistency, about 1 to 2 cups. You may use part milk.

Wash the barley well in lukewarm water, rinse several times. Then cook it very slowly for 3 hours in 1 pint of the white stock into which you have cut the stalk of celery and the leek or onion. When the barley is tender, put the mixture, half at a time, into the blender, or rub through a sieve, until very smooth. Dilute this thick purée with the remaining pint of white stock, heat, and dilute to the desired consistency with the light cream. Taste for seasoning.

AVOCADO SOUP

2 large avocados, mashed well
3 cups Chicken Stock (see recipe)
1½ cups light cream
4 tablespoons sherry
Salt and pepper
1 large avocado, peeled and cut into cubes for garnish

Mash the pulp of the 2 avocados and then rub through a sieve or put into a blender for a few seconds. Combine with the chicken stock and cream. Heat thoroughly but do not boil. Stir in the sherry, season to taste with salt and pepper. Garnish each serving with the avocado cubes.

MINESTRONE

A hearty thick soup that is a meal in itself, minestrone is ideal for lunch or a late supper, needing only crusty bread and a salad.

2 quarts Brown Stock (see recipe)

¼ pound salt pork, cut into 1-inch pieces

¼ pound fresh kidney beans or dried beans that have been soaked for 12 hours

1 cup fresh green peas

2 stalks celery, diced

¼ head small cabbage, shredded

1 cup spinach leaves, shredded

1 large onion, chopped coarsely

2 large carrots, chopped coarsely

2 fresh tomatoes, chopped coarsely

1 sprig or pinch of sage

¼ cup uncooked rice

½ cup uncooked macaroni or spaghetti broken into small pieces

Put 1½ quarts of the stock into a large soup kettle, bring to the boiling point, and then put in all the other ingredients, again bring to the boiling point, lower heat and simmer very gently until vegetables are tender and almost all the stock has been absorbed—about 20 to 30 minutes. Heat the remaining ½ quart of stock and add it. Taste for seasoning. Serve in soup plates and pass a dish of Parmesan cheese to sprinkle on top. This soup is much better if made at least a day in advance and reheated before serving.

FRENCH ONION SOUP

The aroma alone is appetite-provoking. Everyone seems to love French onion soup, but most Americans eat it only on their occasional visit to a French restaurant. This is a pity, for it is almost invariably better when made at home, even if you use canned bouillon instead of homemade brown stock.

4 large onions, thinly sliced	Salt and pepper to taste
4 tablespoons butter	1-inch slices of French bread, toasted
2 quarts Brown Stock (see recipe)	Grated Parmesan cheese to sprinkle on each serving

Sauté the onions in the butter over a low flame until golden brown. Gradually stir in the stock. Season to taste with salt and pepper, cover and simmer gently for 20 minutes. Serve in earthenware soup mugs or in heavy cups. Place a round of toasted French bread in soup mug before pouring in the soup. Sprinkle a generous portion of grated Parmesan on each portion.

LOBSTER BISQUE

Elaborate, yes, but so festive and elegant that it is well worth the trouble, for it elevates the whole meal to epicurean heights. It is especially good if the main course is simple.

1 medium onion, chopped
1 carrot, chopped
1 stalk celery
1 leek, chopped
3 tablespoons olive oil
1½ cups fresh lobster meat
¼ cup cognac
1 cup dry white wine

½ cup rice (do not use converted rice)
1 quart Fish Stock (see recipe)
1 cup heavy cream
3 tablespoons butter
Salt, pepper, and cayenne pepper

Sauté the onion, carrot, celery, and leek in the oil on a low heat for 5 minutes. Add the lobster, cognac, and wine; simmer, covered, for another 5 minutes. Remove the lobster and chop fine. Save the mixture in the pan. Meanwhile, boil the rice in the fish stock until tender, about 20 minutes. Combine the rice and stock mixture with the mixture in which the lobster was cooked and all but ½ cup of the chopped lobster meat. Put into a blender, ⅓ at a time, and blend until smooth. Add the cream and butter and reheat. Add salt, pepper, and cayenne pepper to taste. Garnish each serving with the reserved chopped lobster.

TOMATO SOUP À L'ORANGE

This combination may sound weird, but it is wonderful. The proof of this unusual soup is in the eating. It is best made with fresh vine-ripened tomatoes, but don't restrict yourself to making it only during the tomato season: use canned tomatoes when the fresh are out of season for they are more satisfactory than the expensive hothouse varieties.

2 pounds red ripe tomatoes (or the equivalent amount of canned tomatoes)
1 medium-sized onion, finely sliced
1 medium-sized carrot, finely sliced
1 bay leaf
6 peppercorns

1 strip lemon rind
2½ pints Chicken Stock
2 tablespoons butter
3 tablespoons flour
5 teaspoons sugar
1 cup light cream
Orange peel, finely sliced and blanched

Cut the tomatoes in quarters and squeeze lightly to remove seeds. Do this over a strainer and catch the juice to be used in the soup; discard the seeds. Put the tomatoes, juice and the finely sliced onion and carrot into a stew pan with the bay leaf, peppercorns, lemon rind and stock. If you use canned tomatoes, substitute the liquid for some of the stock. Add a little salt, cover and simmer for half an hour with the lid half-off. Rub through a fine sieve, discard what pulp remains in sieve. Melt the butter in the pan, slowly stir in the flour and then gradually blend in the tomato liquor. This operation can be simplified by using a wire whisk. Add the sugar, and simmer for 5 minutes, or longer if it is necessary to concentrate or thicken the soup a little more. Add the cream, stir, and pour into soup bowls. Garnish with orange rind. This soup may be made in advance and reheated. It freezes well. Defrost and heat. (Garnish does not freeze.)

To prepare the garnish, peel a thick-skinned orange very thinly, with none of the white pith left on the rind. Now slice the rind in long thin slivers. Blanch for four minutes in boiling water and drain. Sprinkle over soup.

HOT WEATHER SOUPS

There is no better way to perk up jaded appetites on a hot sticky day than with a tasty chilled soup. If you own an electric blender, these soups are as effortless to make as to eat. But don't let the lack of a blender deter you from making cold soups, for a fine sieve will do a good job of puréeing, requiring only a little effort to press the vegetables through the sieve. There are, of course, many chilled and jellied consommés which require neither a blender nor a sieve.

VICHYSSOISE

Perhaps the best-known and the most popular of cold soups is vichyssoise, although most people regard it a delicacy to be enjoyed only in a French restaurant. This is regrettable, for it is one of the simplest soups to make at home and ought to be enjoyed frequently during the hot season.

4 medium potatoes, peeled and sliced thin
6 leeks, white part only, sliced thin
1 stalk celery, finely chopped
1 quart White Stock or Chicken Stock (see recipes)
1½ cups light cream
2 tablespoons sherry (optional)
Salt and pepper to taste
Chopped chives for garnish

Boil the potatoes, leeks, and celery in the stock for 20 minutes or until all are very tender. Put them into an electric blender, half at a time, and blend until very smooth. Or rub through a fine sieve. Add the cream, sherry if desired, and season to taste with salt and pepper. Chill the soup. When serving, sprinkle each portion with 1 tablespoon chopped chives.

CHILLED WATERCRESS SOUP

2 tablespoons flour
2 tablespoons butter
1½ cups Chicken Stock (see recipe)
30 sprigs of watercress
¼ medium onion, chopped
½ teaspoon salt
⅛ teaspoon pepper
1 cup milk
1 cup heavy cream

Place the flour, butter, stock, watercress, onion, salt, and pepper into a blender half at a time, and blend until smooth. Transfer to a saucepan and cook, stirring until mixture is thickened. Taste for seasoning. Stir in the milk and cream. Chill thoroughly. Garnish each bowl of soup with a sprig of fresh watercress.

COLD SEAFOOD BISQUE

1½ quarts Fish Stock (see recipe)

4 medium potatoes, peeled and thinly sliced

2 medium onions, thinly sliced

1 bay leaf

¼ teaspoon thyme

¼ teaspoon finely minced garlic

1 teaspoon salt

½ teaspoon pepper

1½ cups mixed seafood: shrimp, scallops, lobster, and crabmeat

2 egg yolks

½ cup light cream

Paprika for garnish

Bring 2 cups of the fish stock to a boil. Add the potatoes, onions, bay leaf, thyme, garlic, salt, and pepper. Simmer for 20 minutes or until vegetables are tender; add the seafood and simmer for another 5 minutes. Remove the bay leaf. Put the mixture in an electric blender, half at a time, and run until smooth or rub through a fine sieve. Return the mixture to pan, add remaining stock and bring to a boil. Taste for seasoning. Remove from heat and gradually stir in the egg yolks mixed with the cream. Chill thoroughly. Sprinkle each serving with paprika.

JELLIED MADRILÈNE

1½ quarts Clarified Stock for Consommé (see recipe)

Lemon slices or wedges for garnish

2 tablespoons gelatin softened in ¼ cup cold water

Heat 2 cups of the consommé to the boiling point and into this stir the softened gelatin, and continue to stir until gelatin is entirely dissolved. Stir in the remaining consommé. Pour into individual bouillon cups and chill until firm. Or, better still, pour into a loaf pan and chill until firm, then cut into cubes and pile into serving cups. Garnish each cup with a thin slice or wedge of lemon.

GAZPACHO

A Spanish soup which is becoming increasingly popular in this country. It is a soup about which people seem to have strong feelings: they either love it or think it inedible. There are many versions of the soup; the following is one of the simplest, but is quite as tasty as the more elaborate ones.

4 *medium onions, thinly sliced*
6 *large tomatoes, peeled and coarsely chopped*
½ *cup red wine*
Salt and pepper to taste
1 *clove garlic, minced*
1 *tablespoon paprika*
2 *tablespoons olive oil*

1 *cucumber*
1 *large tomato, peeled and chopped*
3 *tablespoons finely chopped parsley*
10 *pitted black olives cut into quarters*
Small crisp croutons for garnish

In a saucepan combine the sliced onions and chopped tomatoes, red wine, salt, and pepper. Cook, covered, for 5 minutes or until onion is tender. Add the garlic and paprika and olive oil and put into an electric blender and run for a few seconds or until smooth. Stir in the chopped cucumber, tomato, parsley, and olives. Taste for seasoning. Chill thoroughly. Garnish each portion with tiny crisp croutons.

CHILLED BORSCH

1 quart Brown Stock (see recipe) or use canned beef bouillon
1 bunch raw beets (8 to 10), peeled and grated
½ cup red wine
2 tablespoons tomato paste
1 bay leaf
3 stiffly beaten egg whites
Sour cream and grated lemon rind for garnish

Combine all the ingredients except the sour cream and lemon rind in a kettle and beat with a wire whisk over low heat until it reaches the boiling point. Remove from heat and let stand 15 minutes. Pour through a cheesecloth that has been wrung out in cold water. Taste for seasoning. Chill thoroughly. When serving, pass a bowl of sour cream into which you have mixed grated lemon rind, 2 tablespoons of rind for each cup of sour cream, and let each person garnish his own serving.

JELLIED BORSCH

Make the borsch as in preceding recipe. Soften 2 tablespoons of gelatin in ¼ cup cold water and stir this into the borsch immediately after removing it from the fire, and continue to stir until the gelatin is completely dissolved. Pour the borsch into a loaf pan and chill until firm. Dice and pile into cups. Serve with sour cream and lemon rind.

COLD AVOCADO SOUP

This soup is green, cool, and lovely.

1 large avocado, peeled and quartered
3 cups Chicken Stock (see recipe), or use canned chicken bouillon
1 small clove garlic, pressed
1/8 teaspoon pepper
1/2 cup light cream
Salt to taste
Chives, chopped, for garnish

Put the avocado, 1½ cups of the stock, garlic, and pepper into the blender and run until smooth. Add the remaining stock and cream and blend for another ½ minute. Taste for seasoning. If too thick, add more cream. Chill. When serving, garnish each portion with chopped chives.

In the absence of a blender the avocado can be pressed through a fine sieve and then beaten into the stock with a rotary beater. The garlic can be pressed through a garlic press into the stock.

CHILLED CUCUMBER SOUP

This is my favorite summer soup. Like the Cold Avocado Soup, this soup too is as lovely and cool to look at as it is to eat: pale green flecked with the dark greens of the herbs.

3 cups coarsely chopped peeled cucumber
1½ cups Chicken Stock (see recipe) or use canned broth
1½ cups light cream
1/3 cup chopped chives
1/3 cup chopped celery leaves
4 sprigs of parsley, chopped
3 tablespoons flour
3 tablespoons butter
Grated lemon rind for garnish

Combine all the ingredients and put into an electric blender, half at a time, and run until smooth. Transfer to a saucepan and heat the soup until it reaches the boiling point and is slightly thickened. Taste for seasoning, adding salt and pepper as required. Chill thoroughly. Serve in cups. Garnish with grated lemon rind, about ½ teaspoon of rind for each serving.

Pancakes

"A PANCAKE is a pancake is a pancake" is far from the truth, for the nationality of a pancake makes a distinct difference. There are American pancakes with which you are undoubtedly familiar, a tender, comparatively thick cake, the only pancake which calls for a leavening agent and is baked on a griddle. The pancakes of all other nationalities, although they vary to a slight degree in thickness, have no leavening agent and the batter is much too runny to be baked on a griddle—it must be poured or spooned into a pan the exact size of the pancake you want. There is the French pancake, or crêpe, the thinnest and most elegant of all. It is literally paper-thin and is slightly elastic; it can be handled with ease without breaking. The Russian pancake, or blintz, has the stiffly beaten egg whites folded into the batter, giving the pancake an airier and more tender texture and is, because of the egg white, slightly thicker and much more fragile. The Viennese pancake, or *Palatschinken,* is similar to the crêpe and the blintz and yet quite distinct. It does not have the souffle-like texture of the blintz, nor is it as thin and elastic as the crêpe. It should be about ¼ inch thick and so tender it melts in your mouth. The German pancake, or *Pfann-*

kuchen is a very close relative of the *Palatschinken,* only a bit more eggy. The Hungarian pancake is the same. All of these Continental pancakes can be made with or without sugar and flavoring. If they are to be used in conjunction with meat, fish, or vegetables, they are, of course, unsweetened and unflavored. If they are used with fruit, jam, or a dessert sauce, they have sugar and some flavoring—vanilla, brandy, rum, or a liqueur—added to the batter before frying. The crêpe is undoubtedly best for dessert.

The Russian, Viennese, and German pancakes are excellent with jam, or for brunch or lunch when they double as the main dish and dessert, needing only a salad and beverage to make a pleasant light meal. The Russian blintz is a wonderful lunch or supper dish when stuffed with cottage cheese, refried, and served with sour cream and a tart jam. (The following recipes yield six servings.)

VIENNESE PANCAKE CASSEROLE

Viennese pancakes, unsweetened, layered with a meat, fish, or vegetable filling and baked in a casserole with a sour cream sauce, make an excellent first course for dinner or main course for lunch.

(PALATSCHINKEN) BASIC VIENNESE PANCAKES

1¾ cups flour
2 cups milk
2 egg yolks
¼ teaspoon salt

¼ cup sugar and ½ teaspoon vanilla, if used for dessert or served with jam

Beat the flour and milk until very smooth. Add the egg yolks and salt and blend well. Add sugar and vanilla, if using with fruit or jam. Choose a skillet the size of the pancake you want. These are usually made in an 8-inch pan. Heat the skillet until moderately hot. Brush the surface generously with butter. Pour or spoon in enough of the batter to cover the bottom of skillet, tilt back and forth to spread the batter evenly and thinly. You want the pancake no more than a ¼ inch thick. Fry pancake over moderate heat until lightly browned on bottom, loosen edges with spatula or knife and turn pancake to brown on other side. Invert on to a plate. Repeat with remainder of batter, buttering skillet for each pancake.

Filling

2 tablespoons finely minced onion

1 tablespoon chopped parsley

1 tablespoon butter

1½ cups chopped cooked ham or any other leftover meat, chicken, or seafood

½ cup sautéed mushrooms

1 egg yolk

Salt and pepper to taste (ham needs very little salt, other meats or vegetables need more)

Fry the onions and parsley in hot butter until tender. Add either ham, meat, seafood (or vegetables of your choice), and mushrooms, and blend well. Cool. Add egg yolk and seasoning. Spread mixture on top of each of 6 pancakes. Place one on top of the other in a greased overproof dish.

Sauce

1 cup sour cream

2 egg yolks

Dash salt

Mix well together and pour over the filled and stacked pancakes. Bake at 325° for 30 minutes. Cut into pie-shaped wedges before serving.

PALATSCHINKEN WITH APRICOT JAM

This recipe may be out of place here, as it would never be served as a first course, but it makes such a good light brunch or late after-theater supper that I am including it, along with German Apple Pancakes.

Make a batter according to directions for Basic Viennese Pancakes. Add the sugar and vanilla. Make pancakes in an 8-inch skillet. While one pancake is frying, spread baked pancake with apricot jam, roll, and keep warm in a 300° oven until all are ready. Then sprinkle each pancake generously with coarsely granulated sugar and serve.

(APFEL PFANNKUCHEN) GERMAN APPLE PANCAKES

4 *eggs*	3 *cups thinly sliced apples,*
1 *cup sifted flour*	*sautéed in butter in cov-*
¼ *teaspoon salt*	*ered skillet until tender and*
1 *tablespoon sugar*	*sweetened with sugar*
1½ *cups milk*	*Sugar in shaker*
2 *tablespoons melted butter*	*Cinnamon in shaker*
8 *ounces kirsch*	

Beat eggs lightly, beat in the flour, salt, and sugar, and then stir in the milk and butter. Beat until well-blended and smooth. The batter must be thin enough to spread easily over bottom of pan. Heat a 10-inch skillet, brush the bottom generously with butter, about 3 teaspoons for each pancake, and then pour in enough batter to coat the entire surface, about ⅛ to ¼ inch thick.

As soon as the batter is spread evenly in the skillet, cover it with the sliced apples that have been sautéed in butter in a covered skillet until tender and sweetened to taste with sugar. Unless apples are very tart, add a teaspoon of lemon juice for each cup of apples when sweetening them.

This large pancake isn't as easy to turn as a smaller one, especially when it is covered with apples, so unless you are a master flipper, the best way to turn this pancake is to slide it onto a large dinner plate when the bottom is brown, then add more butter to the pan and flip the cake over back into the pan and brown the second side.

Keep pancakes in a warm oven until all are ready. Now place on a large platter, leaving pancakes flat, sprinkle each one with sugar and cinnamon, and pour the kirsch over all of them, and ignite. When flame dies out, roll each cake, and serve.

CRÊPES

These elegant and famous French pancakes are very useful little items to have in your cooking repertoire. The crêpe is best known as a dessert, especially crêpes Suzette and crêpes Fourrées, but it has many other and more practical uses. Omit the sugar and vanilla from the standard crêpe recipe and you have a pancake to use as the basis for innumerable first-course, luncheon, or supper dishes. The delicate paper-thin pancake can wrap itself around any number of leftovers and make them party fare. The little pancakes can be made in advance and stored in the refrigerator for at least a week or can be frozen and kept indefinitely. It is a good idea to mix up a double batch of the batter, fry 3 or 4 dozen crêpes for use as first courses for luncheon, then add sugar and vanilla to the remaining batter and fry them for use later as desserts.

BASIC CRÊPE RECIPE

1 *cup flour*	3 *tablespoons melted butter*
Pinch salt	(⅛ *cup sugar and ½ tea-*
2 *whole eggs*	*spoon vanilla, if making*
1 *cup ice-cold milk*	*for use as a dessert*)

Sift the flour with the salt into a bowl, break the eggs into the middle, gradually stir in the milk and melted butter, and mix until all the ingredients are well-blended and batter is smooth. Add the sugar and vanilla if using for dessert. Allow batter to stand in refrigerator for an hour before using. When you are ready to fry the crêpes, in a small skillet, just the size of crêpe you want (a 6-inch skillet is best for the dessert crêpe, an 8- to 10-inch skillet for others), heat a little butter until sizzling, pour in a tablespoon or two of batter depending on size of pan, and tilt the pan so that the batter spreads evenly over the entire surface. The crêpe must be paper-thin. If batter is too thick, add a bit more milk. When delicately brown on one side, turn and allow the other side to brown. This process takes only a minute for each crêpe. It should not be necessary to butter the pan for each crêpe. In fact, after the first two or three the pan should be sufficiently greased to fry the remainder without additional butter. This depends, of course, on how well-seasoned your pan is.

CRÊPES NIÇOISES WITH CRABMEAT

Have three or four unsweetened crêpes for each person to be served. (See Basic Crêpe Recipe.)

½ pound mushrooms, coarsely chopped

3 tablespoons butter

2 cups finely shredded cooked crabmeat

1 tablespoon chopped parsley

4 tablespoons Sauce (recipe below), or enough to bind the mixture together

Remaining Sauce to cover and Parmesan cheese to sprinkle on top

Sauté the mushrooms in the butter until tender, or about 4 minutes. Add the crabmeat, parsley, and sauce, and mix well together.

Divide this mixture among the pancakes, roll up each pancake, and arrange on a large flat serving dish and pour the Sauce (see below) over all. Sprinkle the top of each crêpe generously with grated Parmesan cheese and drip butter over them. Put under a hot broiler until delicately brown.

The whole dish may be made in advance, in which case reheat in a 375° oven for 10 minutes, or until heated through, before putting under the broiler to brown.

Sauce

3 tablespoons butter

4 tablespoons flour

2 cups Fish Stock (see recipe)

⅔ cup light cream

2 egg yolks

2 tablespoons sherry

Melt the butter in a pan, stir in the flour. When well-mixed, gradually stir in the Fish Stock. Stir with a wire whisk over low heat until thickened and smooth. Stir in the light cream. Carefully add a bit of the hot mixture to the beaten yolks, warming them slowly so that they will not curdle when added to the sauce. Add the yolks and sherry and heat through but do not boil.

VARIATIONS: Substitute shredded cooked chicken, veal, ham, tongue, or any combination of these for the crabmeat in the preceding recipe, and substitute Chicken Stock for the Fish Stock in the sauce. Except for these substitutions, proceed as directed.

CRÊPES WITH PURÉED SPINACH

Allow 3 or 4 crêpes for each serving (see Basic Crêpe Recipe). Fill each crêpe with Puréed Spinach and roll, arranging them on a flat serving dish. Sprinkle with Parmesan cheese, or cover with a Suprême Sauce (see below) and then sprinkle with Parmesan, brown under the broiler, and serve hot.

Puréed Spinach

2 *pounds fresh spinach, or
2 packages frozen spinach,
cooked until just tender*

*and sautéed in butter until
tender*
½ *cup sour cream*
Salt and pepper

1 *medium onion, minced fine*

Drain the cooked spinach thoroughly and put into an electric blender, or press through a food mill or sieve, to get a fine purée. Mix in the sautéed onion and sour cream, and season to taste.

Served on thin slices of baked ham, these crêpes make an excellent main course for lunch or supper.

Suprême Sauce

2 *tablespoons butter*
3 *tablespoons flour*
1 *cup veal or Chicken Stock
(this may be made with
bouillon cubes or other
stock base)*

⅓ *cup cream or milk*
1 *egg yolk*
1 *teaspoon lemon juice*
Salt and pepper to taste

Melt the butter, add flour gradually, and stir until well blended. Add stock slowly, stirring constantly with a wire whisk until boiling point is reached. Turn down fire and simmer for 2 minutes. Mix the egg yolk with the cream and gradually stir into the sauce. Do not permit it to boil after the addition of the egg yolk. Add lemon juice and season to taste with salt and pepper.

CRÊPES WITH PAPRIKA MUSHROOMS

Allow 3 or 4 crêpes for each person. (See Basic Crêpe Recipe.)

Divide the Paprika Mushrooms among the crêpes, roll each crêpe and arrange on a serving dish, brush with melted butter, and brown under the broiler.

4 tablespoons butter	½ teaspoon salt
1 large onion, finely chopped	½ teaspoon pepper
1½ pounds mushrooms,	1 teaspoon rose paprika
thinly sliced	2 tablespoons flour
1½ cups sour cream	

Melt the butter and sauté the onion until golden. Add the sliced mushrooms and cook for 4 or 5 minutes, or until tender. Stir in the seasoning and flour, cook for another 5 minutes. Stir in the sour cream, heat, but do not allow it to boil.

These paprika mushrooms are equally delicious served in a patty shell or on a round of toast.

Artichokes

THE ARTICHOKE is an aristocrat among vegetables. It is
better served as a dish in itself than as an accompaniment
to a main dish. There are many ways of dressing up this
elegant vegetable. I will give two below, but it is not necessary to give artichokes fancy treatment to make a delicious
dish.

ARTICHOKES WITH BUTTER

6 *large firm artichokes*   *Melted butter, with a squeeze*
Court bouillon for boiling   *of lemon juice*
   them

Boil the artichokes in the court bouillon for 30 to 45
minutes or until leaves come out easily. Prepare the court
bouillon by adding to the pan of cooking water, salt, 1
sliced onion, stalk of celery, bay leaf, 2 slices of lemon,
and a sliced carrot.

Drain the artichokes well, place on individual serving
plates and accompany each plate with a small dish of
melted butter to which you have added a squeeze of lemon

juice. If you have small burners to keep the butter hot, all the better.

COLD ARTICHOKES WITH MAYONNAISE OR VINAIGRETTE SAUCE

Boil artichokes as in preceding recipe, drain, and chill. Place on individual serving plates, and pass a bowl of homemade Mayonnaise (see recipe) or a small pitcher of Vinaigrette Sauce. To prepare Vinaigrette Sauce: mix together 2 tablespoons vinegar with 6 tablespoons olive oil and add ½ teaspoon prepared mustard, salt to taste, and 1 tablespoon mixed chopped herbs: parsley, tarragon, chervil, and chives.

STUFFED ARTICHOKES

6 *large firm artichokes*
3 *tablespoons butter*
½ *pound mushrooms, finely chopped*
⅔ *cup shredded cooked meat, ham, tongue, or chicken*
2 *shallots, finely chopped or 2 tablespoons minced onion*
1 *tablespoon tomato purée*

3 *tablespoons chopped parsley*
½ *cup fine dry bread crumbs*
3 *tablespoons olive oil*
½ *cup white wine and 2 tablespoons sherry*
½ *cup chicken stock or bouillon*
2 *tablespoons butter*

2 *tablespoons flour*

Cut one inch from the tops of the artichokes and remove the tough outside leaves. Boil the artichokes according to directions on page 37. Place upside down on rack to drain thoroughly, and when cool enough to handle, pull out the very middle leaves and remove the choke.

Melt 3 tablespoons butter in a saucepan, sauté the

mushrooms for 3 minutes, add the shredded meat and the shallots. Stir in the tomato purée, parsley, and 2 tablespoons of the bread crumbs; cook, stirring for 3 minutes.

Now stuff the artichokes with this mixture and sprinkle the tops with the remaining crumbs. Set them in a greased baking dish, near enough together so that they will not spread and fall apart while baking. Pour the olive oil, white wine, sherry, and stock around them. Cover the dish and bake at 350° for 45 minutes. Arrange on a dish and keep warm.

Melt 2 tablespoons butter in a small pan, blend in the flour and gradually add the liquor from the baking dish. Cook, stirring, until smooth and thickened. Pour this sauce around the artichokes on the serving plate.

Mushrooms

FRESH MUSHROOMS are a delicacy that are within the means of almost everyone. However, although the preparation of them can be simple, and with delightful results, some people never use mushrooms, and many others use only canned mushrooms. Too often, many of those who do use mushrooms tend to cook them only as one ingredient among many in a dish. Mushrooms do, of course, make a wonderful addition to innumerable dishes, but they are superb as a dish in themselves, or as the main ingredients of a dish, as in Crêpes with Paprika Mushrooms (see recipe).

The following recipes yield six servings.

MUSHROOMS UNDER GLASS

A most elegant way to begin a dinner is with mushrooms under glass. Even when they are followed by a simple main course, the guests will go away feeling they have dined like gourmets. Don't let the absence of glass domes deter you from trying this recipe, for you can put 6 mounds of mushrooms on a 10-inch pie plate and invert a 10-inch glass casserole over them, or use two 7- or 8-inch plates and the corresponding glass casseroles inverted for covers. They are, however, much more impressive-looking if served under individual glass bells. These can be purchased in the houseware departments of the better stores, or in shops that specialize in fancy houseware and kitchenware, or in hotel supply houses.

1½ pounds mushrooms, 6 large, the rest medium and small
½ cup soft butter
4 teaspoons lemon juice
2 tablespoons chopped parsley
1 teaspoon salt
2 teaspoons rose paprika
6 rounds of toast
¾ cup cream
3 tablespoons sherry

Trim stems from mushrooms. Wash and dry the caps. Cream butter and add lemon juice, parsley, salt, and paprika. Spread the cooled toast rounds with ½ of the butter mixture and place either in individual baking dishes or in a large pie plate. Spread the remaining butter mixture on the mushroom caps. Heap the mushrooms on the toast rounds, placing a large mushroom on the bottom and pyramiding the remaining mushrooms on top. Pour cream over the mounds of mushrooms, cover with individual glass domes or with a large glass dome or inverted glass casserole. Bake for 15 minutes at 375°. Just before serving, lift covers and pour ½ tablespoon sherry on each mound.

MUSHROOMS STUFFED WITH CRABMEAT

This is even better than it sounds, and it does sound delicious.

6 tablespoons butter
3 tablespoons flour
1 cup chicken broth
½ cup heavy cream
Salt, pepper, and cayenne pepper to taste
2 tablespoons chopped shallots or onions
1 teaspoon dry mustard

¾ pound crabmeat
4 tablespoons sherry
2 hard-boiled eggs, chopped
1 tablespoon chopped chives
1 tablespoon chopped parsley
18 good-sized mushrooms
¾ cup buttered fresh bread crumbs

Melt 3 tablespoons butter in a saucepan, add the flour, and cook, stirring with a wire whisk for 3 minutes, without letting the flour brown. Bring the chicken broth to the boil and to it add the flour mixture, stirring constantly with a whisk. Heat the heavy cream and stir it in. Season to taste with salt, pepper, and cayenne. In a small skillet melt 1 tablespoon butter and sauté the chopped shallot or onion until transparent. Add the dry mustard and let it simmer for a few seconds. Add the crabmeat, and when it is heated, add the sherry. Combine the crab mixture with the sauce, and add the chopped eggs, chives, and parsley.

Remove the stems from the mushrooms and sauté the mushrooms in the remaining butter for 5 minutes.

Fill each mushroom cavity with the crab, dividing the mixture evenly among the mushrooms. Sprinkle with the bread crumbs and bake at 450° for 8 minutes. Serve the mushrooms on a bed of wild rice or on buttered toast rounds.

Egg Dishes

IN AMERICA the egg is food for breakfast, generally speaking. It is, to be sure, an excellent way to start the day, but it is really scandalous to neglect using this versatile food for other meals. The soufflé, belatedly achieving popularity in this country, is just one of many ways to bring egg dishes into lunch and dinner menus. The soufflé recipes that follow can be made even by an amateur cook without mishap. And once you master the technique of one soufflé, you can invent variations practically without limit. The other egg dishes given below are so delicious that, having tried these, you might feel inspired to seek other new and exciting ways to use the humble egg. All recipes serve six.

MUSHROOM SOUFFLÉ

Soufflés make an excellent luncheon dish and are justly popular as such, but they serve equally well as a first course.

2 *tablespoons butter*
3 *tablespoons flour*
¼ *teaspoon salt and small pinch cayenne pepper*
¾ *cup milk*
2 *tablespoons grated cheddar*

or Parmesan cheese
4 *egg yolks*
1 *cup sliced mushrooms sautéed in butter until tender, or about 4 minutes*
5 *stiffly beaten egg whites*

Melt butter, stir in flour, salt, and cayenne. Gradually pour on the milk, stirring constantly with a wire whisk until thickened and smooth. Add the grated cheese, beaten egg yolks, and mushrooms. Warm the egg yolks slightly with some of the hot mixture before adding. Fold in the stiffly beaten egg whites. Grease a 7-inch soufflé dish and also grease a 4-inch-wide strip of aluminum foil and wrap it around the top of the dish to form a high collar, making the dish at least 2 inches higher. Pour in the mixture and bake at 400° for 35 minutes. Remove the collar and serve immediately.

BROCCOLI OR SPINACH SOUFFLÉ

Substitute 1 cup cooked chopped broccoli or 1 cup cooked chopped spinach for the mushrooms in the preceding recipe.

CHEESE SOUFFLÉ

Substitute ⅔ cup grated Swiss cheese for the mushrooms in the recipe for Mushroom Soufflé (see recipe), and use 3 tablespoons Parmesan cheese instead of 2.

EGGS FLORENTINE

A very pretty and tasty way to serve eggs and to get a meal off to a good start.

2 pounds spinach
1 tablespoon butter
¼ teaspoon salt and dash pepper
4 tablespoons sour cream
6 eggs poached
2 tablespoons butter
3 tablespoons flour
1 cup milk
3 tablespoons grated Swiss cheese
2 tablespoons grated Parmesan cheese
½ teaspoon dry mustard
¼ cup light cream
1 egg yolk

Wash spinach well and put into a saucepan with 1 tablespoon butter, the salt, and pepper. Cook for 5 minutes, stirring occasionally, drain well, and chop into a fine purée or put into a blender for a few seconds. Mix in the sour cream and arrange on a serving dish. Arrange the poached eggs in an attractive pattern on top of the spinach and cover with Sauce (directions below). Make the Sauce (see below) before putting the dish together. The spinach can be made in advance and reheated, the eggs must be poached at the last minute. Break each egg into a small dish and slip it carefully into rapidly boiling water into which you have added a few drops of vinegar.

To make the Sauce: Melt the butter in a pan, stir in the flour, and gradually pour in the milk, stirring constantly with a wire whisk until thickened and smooth. Add salt and pepper to taste. Add the cheese, mustard, and cream. Simmer for 5 minutes. Mix a little of the hot mixture with the egg yolk and then carefully stir the egg yolk into the sauce. Pour the sauce over the poached eggs, sprinkle the top with Parmesan cheese, and brown under the broiler.

SOUFFLÉ ROLL WITH HAM FILLING

This beautiful roll is complicated-looking, but it's even easier to make than a regular soufflé. It is an extremely handy item to have in your cooking files, for it lends itself to disguising any number of leftovers, since the filling can be made from dabs of this or that and emerge as party fare. It can be made a day in advance.

5 tablespoons butter	5 egg yolks
½ cup plus 2 tablespoons flour	1 teaspoon sugar
2¼ cups milk	5 egg whites, stiffly beaten
	Pinch salt

Grease a 10- by 15-inch cookie sheet or jelly roll pan, line it with waxed paper, and grease again. Dust lightly with flour.

In a saucepan melt the butter, flour, and salt, and stir with a wire whisk until well blended. Gradually stir in the milk and cook, stirring, for 3 or 4 minutes, until smooth and thick. Remove from the fire and blend in the slightly beaten egg yolks and sugar, warming them first with a little of the hot mixture. Fold in the egg whites. Spread the batter evenly on the greased and paper-lined sheet and bake at 325° for 45 minutes. Turn the pan over onto a sheet of waxed paper, lift off the pan and carefully peel off the paper from the bottom of the soufflé. Cool. Spread the roll with the filling and roll it up with the help of the waxed paper, turning it gently onto itself. Serve on a long wooden board if you have one, otherwise on a long platter.

Ham Filling

2 cups cooked ham, finely chopped or minced	¼ cup chopped chives
	½ teaspoon dijon mustard
1 cup sour cream	

Mix all ingredients together and spread on the roll.

VARIATIONS: Should your refrigerator have some leftover chicken or turkey or, perhaps, shrimp, crab, or lobster, any of these can be substituted for the ham. (In the case of seafood, use mayonnaise instead of sour cream.) Another very good filling is a mixture of cream cheese, sour cream, and caviar, either red or black. For each ½ cup of caviar, use 3 ounces cream cheese and ⅓ cup sour cream.

EGGS MOLLET À L'INDIENNE

This may not be everyone's egg dish, but for those who like East Indian cooking or who like odd combinations, I recommend this as a first course or a luncheon dish on a summer day.

6 *eggs*
1 *cup rice*
Curry Cream Dressing

Curry Cream Dressing

1 *teaspoon curry powder*
1 *finely chopped onion*
1 *teaspoon olive oil*
½ *teaspoon paprika*
¼ *cup tomato juice*
¼ *cup white wine*

1 *cup mayonnaise*
2 *tablespoons sieved apricot jam or jelly*
2 *or more tablespoons heavy cream*

Place the eggs in boiling water and boil for 5 minutes. Put immediately into cold water and leave 8 minutes, then peel carefully and slip into fresh cold water until wanted.

Boil the rice until tender. If you use converted rice you will have no trouble obtaining rice that is dry and fluffy. Drain and allow to dry thoroughly.

Meanwhile cook the curry powder and chopped onion in the oil until the onion is soft and golden; add the paprika, tomato juice, and wine, cook for 6 minutes and then strain. Cool and stir in the mayonnaise and apricot jam. Taste for seasoning, adding salt if necessary and more jam if you desire. Now stir in the cream to mellow the mixture.

Arrange the rice down the center of a serving dish. Dry the eggs carefully and place on top of the rice in a neat row or double row. Spoon the curry cream dressing over the eggs, and garnish with strips of pimento and a light sprinkling of paprika.

EGGS EN CROUSTADE WITH SPINACH

This recipe takes more time in the telling than it does in the making. Don't let the fact that the recipe is in several parts deter you from trying it, for it is well worth what effort it does involve. It is attractive to serve and delightful to eat. Double the recipe and have a most happy answer for a lunch or supper menu.

Short Crust pastry (*see recipe*   6 *poached eggs*
   in PIES AND TARTS *section**)   1 *pound Puréed Spinach*
           Cheese Sauce

Puréed Spinach

1 *pound spinach*   *Pinch salt*
1 *tablespoon onion, finely*
chopped

Wash and cook spinach until barely tender, or about 4 minutes. Drain thoroughly. Put into a blender and twirl until puréed, or chop finely with sharp knife. Add chopped onion that has been sautéed until golden, add salt. Mix well.

*Omit sugar

Cheese Sauce

2 *tablespoons butter*
3 *tablespoons flour*
2 *cups milk*

¾ *cup grated cheese (sharp cheddar or a mixture of Swiss and Parmesan*

Pinch salt

Melt the butter in a pan, stir in the flour and then gradually stir in the milk, using a wire whisk to obtain a smooth sauce more easily. When thickened and smooth, add ½ cup of the grated cheese. Save the remaining cheese to sprinkle on top. This sauce may be made ahead of time and reheated before using.

Now cover the bottom of each tart shell with the puréed spinach. Carefully place a well-drained poached egg on top of the spinach, spoon over the sauce, and sprinkle top with cheese. Brown quickly under the broiler.

Fish and Shellfish

IN NO CATEGORY of cooking is the Continental way more exciting, compared to the American way, than in that of fish and shellfish. With such an abundance of fine fish and shellfish obtainable in this country it is surprising that so few have learned what others have to teach us about cooking this oldest of foods.

Fish and shellfish adapt well to first courses and to lunch and supper main dishes: they are easy to dress up elegantly, and deliciously, to set the tone for a formal dinner; they make an attractive and satisfying main course at lunch or supper. The possibilities are legion. Given below are recipes which, it is hoped, will demonstrate the ease and excitement of serving fish and shellfish in a variety of ways. May these encourage you to add interest to your table by hunting out still more delicious and attractive ways to serve them. The recipes yield six servings.

SOLE IN WHITE WINE

This is a basic recipe for preparing sole. On this foundation can be built many sole dishes by merely adding additional ingredients to the sauce or by varying the garnishes. Grated cheese added to the sauce will give you Sole Mornay; blanched white grapes, Sole Veronique; or garnish with a variety of seafood such as mussels, shrimp, and oysters and you have Sole Normande. Or add 3 tablespoons of lobster butter to the sauce and garnish with slices of cooked lobster and you have Sole Cardinal.

6 *fillets of sole*	1 *bay leaf*
½ *cup white wine*	2 *slices of onion*
½ *cup Fish Stock (see recipe)*	Salt and pepper

Wash and dry the sole. Salt and pepper each fillet, fold over neatly, and arrange side by side in a well-buttered ovenproof dish. Pour over the wine, stock, bay leaf, and onion. Cover with waxed paper and poach for 20 minutes in a 350° oven. Carefully pour off the liquor and save for the Sauce. Keep fillets warm in the oven.

Sauce

2 *tablespoons butter*	½ *cup cream*
2 *tablespoons flour*	1 *egg yolk*
1 *cup of the fish liquor*	Salt and pepper to taste

Melt the butter in a pan. Stir in the flour. When the roux is well blended but before it takes on any color, gradually stir in the fish stock. Use a wire whisk to get a smooth sauce. Simmer for 3 or 4 minutes, stirring, and then gradually add the cream. Beat the egg yolk slightly, and after warming it with a bit of the hot liquid, stir it into the sauce. Do not permit to boil. Coat the fillets with the sauce and glaze quickly under a hot broiler. Serve as is or garnish as your mood dictates.

CROUSTADE DE SOLE

6 *fillets of sole, poached for 15 minutes according to directions in preceding recipe*
3 *tablespoons Béchamel Sauce (see recipe)*
4 *tablespoons grated Parmesan cheese*

3 *tablespoons grated Swiss cheese*
¼ *teaspoon salt*
Dash cayenne
2 *egg yolks*
4 *egg whites, stiffly beaten*

Combine the Béchamel Sauce with the grated cheese, salt, and cayenne. Stir in the beaten egg yolks and then fold in the egg whites.

Lift the fillets out of the liquid and arrange on a shallow ovenproof dish that can be brought to the table. Divide the soufflé mixture among the six fillets, covering the fish completely and mounding the soufflé mixture attractively. Sprinkle the top with additional grated Parmesan. Bake at 400° for 10 minutes, or until puffed and golden brown. Serve with a hollandaise sauce.

BÉCHAMEL SAUCE

An authentic Béchamel Sauce is so much better than quick substitutes for it that it is well worth the extra time it takes to make it. It can be made in large quantities and stored in the refrigerator up to a week, or it can be put into half pint and pint containers and frozen, ready to use in the amount you need.

5 *tablespoons butter*
1 *medium-sized onion,*
  chopped
½ *cup flour*
1 *quart hot milk*
4 *ounces veal, cut into*
  small pieces

⅛ *teaspoon thyme*
Pinch nutmeg
Pinch pepper
½ *teaspoon salt*

Melt 4 tablespoons butter in the top part of a double boiler directly over the heat. Add the chopped onion and cook until soft; do not brown. Stir in the flour, gradually add the hot milk, and cook, stirring with a wire whisk until thickened and smooth. (The onions will, of course, give it a somewhat lumpy appearance.) Remove this mixture from the heat while you simmer the veal in 1 tablespoon of butter 4 minutes, after which add the remaining ingredients to the veal. Then add the veal to the sauce, and place sauce over boiling water. Cook covered for 1 hour. Strain sauce to remove the onion and veal, and you will have a smooth, thick Béchamel. If the sauce is too thick for any one particular use, thin it down to desired consistency with cream or milk. When using sauce that has been stored, reheat the amount you need, thin if necessary, and gradually stir in 1 egg yolk for every one to two cups of sauce.

QUICK BÉCHAMEL SAUCE

There are occasions when you haven't any Béchamel Sauce on hand and haven't the time to make it, so a recipe is given below for an acceptable, quickly made version.

2 *cups milk*	¼ *cup flour*
1 *bay leaf*	1 *egg yolk, mixed with*
Large slice onion	1 *tablespoon cream*
2 *tablespoons butter*	*Dash nutmeg*
	Salt and pepper

Add onion and bay leaf to milk and heat slowly. Meanwhile melt butter in a saucepan and stir in flour, adding it gradually. When this roux is well blended, stir in the heated milk (from which bay leaf and onion have been strained out) and cook, stirring with a wire whisk, until sauce is thickened and smooth. Warm the egg yolk and cream with a bit of the hot sauce, and then carefully stir it into the sauce. Add nutmeg and season to taste with salt and pepper.

COQUILLES SAINT JACQUES

This is a tasty and attractive way to begin a meal, or double the portions and lunch like an epicure.

The Coquilles Saint Jacques is a famous French dish and one most American visitors to France have eaten. Americans, however, do not have to go to France to enjoy this delicacy for it is easily made at home.

"Coquille" means shell, and large shells should be used in serving this dish, if you believe, as I do, that eye appeal is very important in food. Large scallop shells can be purchased in most houseware or fancy food shops, but you can save money and have fun by picking up your own shells on one of your excursions to the beach.

STANDARD COQUILLES SAINT JACQUES

1½ pounds deep-sea
  scallops
1 cup white wine
½ cup water
2 cups Mornay Sauce
  (recipe below)
1 cup thinly sliced mush-
  rooms

1 tablespoon minced onion
  sautéed in butter until tender, or about 4 minutes
Buttered bread crumbs mixed
  with Parmesan cheese to
  sprinkle on top of each
  coquille

Parboil the scallops in the wine and water for 5 minutes,
or until barely tender. The liquid should just cover the
scallops (usually about 1½ cups). If more is necessary,
add wine and water, using 2 parts wine to 1 part water.
Drain and reserve the liquid. If liquid exceeds 1 cup, reduce it to 1 cup by boiling over medium heat.

MORNAY SAUCE

3 tablespoons butter
3 tablespoons flour
½ teaspoon salt
⅛ teaspoon pepper
⅔ cup milk
1 cup liquid from the
  scallops

4 tablespoons grated Swiss
  cheese or sharp cheddar
2 egg yolks
½ cup cream
2 tablespoons sherry

Melt the butter in a pan, stir in the flour, and blend
thoroughly, but do not brown. Add the salt and pepper,
and then, gradually, while stirring with a wire whisk,
pour in the milk and liquid from the scallops. Cook,
stirring constantly, until sauce is thickened and smooth,
and then stir in the grated cheese. Now mix the egg yolks
with the cream, and after warming it by stirring in a bit
of the hot sauce, carefully add it to the sauce. Heat but
do not permit it to boil. Stir in the sherry.

If the scallops are large, slice each into three slices. If small bay scallops are used, leave whole.

Now mix the scallops, Mornay sauce, and the sautéed mushrooms and onions. Taste for seasoning. Fill the individual shells, sprinkle the top of each with a mixture of buttered bread crumbs and Parmesan cheese, and put under a hot broiler until delicately brown.

If you make the coquilles in advance, and they have cooled or even become cold from being stored in the refrigerator, put them in a hot oven for 5 minutes to heat through before browning under the broiler.

VARIATION ON COQUILLES SAINT JACQUES

Substitute other seafood for part of the scallops. Shrimp, lobster, crab, clams, or oysters can be substituted, or various combinations of these. If clams or oysters are used, reserve their liquor and add it to the sauce. Parboil the clams and oysters with the scallops for only the last minute of cooking. If shrimp and lobster are used, cook them in a court bouillon for 15 minutes, then shell and clean. If fresh crabmeat is used, bone and then place in a pan with ½ cup of white wine and simmer for 5 minutes.

COQUILLES À LA BRETONNE

These coquilles are a bit simpler to prepare in that there is no separate sauce.

1½ pounds scallops
3 tablespoons finely chopped onion
1 clove garlic finely minced
4 tablespoons butter
4 tablespoons white wine
1 tablespoon chopped parsley
⅓ cup fine dry bread crumbs
2 tablespoons melted butter
3 tablespoons bread crumbs for topping

Cut the scallops into small pieces, combine with the chopped onion and garlic. Melt the 4 tablespoons butter in a skillet and add the scallops and onion mixture. Fry quickly for 2 or 3 minutes. Add the wine and parsley. Mix in the bread crumbs and simmer gently for 2 minutes. Now spoon the mixture into scallop shells, sprinkle the top with dry bread crumbs and the melted butter. Bake in a 500° oven for 2 or 3 minutes.

PIKE QUENELLES

Of all quenelles, pike quenelles are the most ambrosial. But you must have the patience of an angel to make them. There is no fast and easy way to produce a good quenelle, and a bad quenelle is far worse than none. But—a properly prepared quenelle is truly food for the gods.

First make a Fish Stock (see recipe) unless you already have some in your refrigerator or freezer.

Then make a paste of:

½ cup plus 2 tablespoons flour	Dash nutmeg
2 egg yolks	½ stick butter (¼ cup), melted
½ teaspoon each, salt and pepper	6 tablespoons milk, boiling

Mix the flour, egg yolks, and seasoning in a pan. Add the melted butter and, slowly, the boiling milk. Stir over low heat until smooth and very thick, rather globby-looking. You may add an extra tablespoon of milk if necessary to bind it together. Let cook.

Now prepare the pike.

1 pound pike meat (2 pounds of pike will yield this; use the bones in making the stock)	2 egg whites
	1 teaspoon salt
	Dash pepper and nutmeg
	2 cups heavy cream

Pound and mix the pike meat. You may run it through a food chopper and then put it into a blender. Then blend in ½ egg white at a time. Add the seasonings. When very smooth, add the cooled paste and mix very thoroughly. Then force through a sieve or food mill. Let cool over ice in the refrigerator for 1 hour.

Take the heavy cream, whip ⅔ of it until about half as thick as you usually whip cream. Add the unwhipped cream little by little to the pike mixture, keeping the bowl over ice the whole time. Then work in the partially whipped cream until it is all absorbed. The mixture should now be smooth as satin and light and airy. Keep cool until ready to poach.

Put the Fish Stock in a large deep skillet on top of stove and bring to a boil. With two spoons take out the pike mixture and try to get a cylindrical shape as you drop it into the simmering stock. Put in three or four at a time, cover, and poach for 3 or 4 minutes. Lift out ever so gently and drain. Put into a shallow baking dish. When all the quenelles are poached, drain the stock and use to make a Fish Velouté Sauce (see below) to pour over them. Place under the broiler for a few seconds and serve.

FISH VELOUTÉ SAUCE

2 tablespoons butter
2 tablespoons flour
1 cup Fish Stock (see recipe) or clam juice

1 egg yolk
½ cup cream

Melt butter in a pan, stir in the flour. When well-blended, gradually stir in the fish stock or clam juice, using a wire whisk. When thickened and smooth, simmer gently for 3 minutes. Combine the egg yolk and cream, and then stir a little of the hot mixture into the cream mixture before carefully adding it to the sauce. Do not permit it to boil.

STUFFED CLAMS

2 *dozen clams*
1 *tablespoon finely chopped onion*
1 *tablespoon chopped parsley*
1 *tablespoon chopped tarragon (or ½ teaspoon dried tarragon)*
½ *cup buttered bread crumbs*
1 *cup Fish Velouté Sauce (see recipe), or enough to bind the mixture together*
Salt and pepper to taste
Few grains cayenne
1 *tablespoon sherry*
Buttered bread crumbs to sprinkle top

Scrub the clams. Then place them in a large kettle with ½ inch of salted water. Cover tightly and allow to steam until clams open, or 5 to 10 minutes.

Remove clams from their shells, saving the bottom shell. Chop clams fine and mix with the onion, parsley, tarragon, bread crumbs, and enough Fish Velouté Sauce to hold the mixture together. Taste for seasoning. Stir in the sherry. Pile the mixture into the reserved shells, sprinkle with the buttered bread crumbs and brown quickly under the broiler. If made in advance, put the shells into a hot oven for 3 minutes to heat through before browning under the broiler.

CLAMS WITH CREAM

3 *dozen hard-shell clams*
1 *cup water*
1½ *tablespoons chopped shallot or onion*
1 *small clove garlic minced*
1 *tablespoon butter*
½ *cup dry white wine*
½ *cup heavy cream or sour cream*
Salt to taste
Dash of cayenne pepper
2 *eggs yolks, beaten*

Put the clams into a kettle with 1 cup of water. Steam until shells open. Remove clams from kettle, save the liquid. Discard the top shell.

Sauté the shallot or onion and garlic in butter until soft but not brown. Add the dry white wine and the reserved liquid from the clams. Simmer for 2 minutes. Stir in the cream. Season to taste. Warm the beaten egg yolks with a bit of the hot mixture and then gradually stir them into the sauce. Stir over low heat until thickened and smooth, but do not permit sauce to boil. Pour the sauce over the clams on the half shell and serve hot.

CRAB WITH ALMONDS

This is very similar to crab imperial, but, I think, even more delightful. It goes together easily but makes a most impressive appearance.

⅓ cup butter
1 cup sliced blanched
  almonds
¼ cup finely chopped onion
¼ cup coarsely chopped
  green pepper
2 cups crab meat
1 can mushroom soup

Salt and pepper to taste
Dash Worcestershire
1 teaspoon dry mustard
3 tablespoons sherry
1 cup thick white sauce, or
  Fish Velouté Sauce (see
  recipe)

Heat the butter until it bubbles. Add the almonds and brown lightly. Watch the almonds closely, for they quickly pass the light brown stage and become too dark. Remove the almonds from the skillet, and, if necessary, add a bit more butter and sauté the onion and green pepper until tender. Add the crab meat and turn off the heat. Stir in the salt, pepper, Worcestershire, mustard, sherry, and almonds. Blend in the white sauce and mushroom soup. Put into individual shells or ramekins or in one large flat baking dish and bake for 20 minutes at 350°. If not attractively brown on top after this time in the oven, put it under the broiler to brown. If dish is made ahead of time and kept in the refrigerator, it will need at least another 10 minutes in the oven.

SHRIMP ITALIAN

Shrimp lends itself well to setting a tone for a dinner, and equally well to being the mainstay at lunch or supper. This dish is simplicity itself to prepare, attractive to serve, and most satisfying to eat.

½ cup butter
2 cloves garlic minced
3 tablespoons parsley, finely chopped
¼ teaspoon paprika
1 teaspoon grated lemon peel

1 teaspoon summer savory
1 cup fine dry bread crumbs
¼ cup grated Parmesan
¼ cup sherry
2 pounds shrimp, shelled and deveined

Melt the butter in a skillet, cook the garlic until yellow. Add parsley, paprika, lemon peel, and savory. Stir and cook for 3 minutes. Add the crumbs and Parmesan cheese and mix well. Arrange the shrimp in a greased shallow casserole. Cover with the mixture and sprinkle the sherry over top. Bake at 325° for 25 minutes or until golden.

SHRIMP BUONGUSTO

Shrimp in a light highly flavored sauce makes an excellent introduction to a dinner. The shrimp are low in calories and the light sauce is tasty rather than filling, a dish to stimulate the appetite not satisfy it. Serve in small individual casseroles or on thin slices of crisp toast.

2 *pounds shrimp, shelled* *and deveined*
Flour for dredging
¼ *cup olive oil*
3 *tablespoons butter*
1 *large clove garlic*
¾ *cup dry white wine plus* 2 *tablespoons sherry*

1 *tablespoon tomato paste*
4 *tablespoons warm water*
½ *teaspoon salt*
½ *teaspoon pepper*
Dash cayenne pepper
2 *tablespoons chopped* *parsley*
2 *tablespoons minced onion*

1 *tablespoon lemon juice*

Wash and dry the shrimp and dredge lightly in flour. Put the olive oil and butter in a pan with the clove of garlic cut in half, and when foaming, add the shrimp and sauté until golden, or about 3 minutes. Remove the oil and butter from pan and save. Discard garlic. Add wine and sherry to shrimp and cook until wine has reduced by two-thirds, or about 4 minutes. Place the oil in a small pan with the tomato paste, water, salt, pepper, and cayenne and cook for 4 minutes. Pour over the shrimp, add the parsley and minced onion, and simmer for 4 minutes. Add lemon juice and serve.

CRAB BRAQUES OR TARTS

The small boat-shaped tart pans make this dish a bit more attractive, but the round 3-inch tart pans do perfectly well. These fragrant little crab-filled pastries are so delicious that they would be well-received in any shape or form.

Short Crust pastry (see recipe *in* PIES AND TARTS *section*)*
3 *tablespoons grated* *Parmesan*
⅛ *pound flaked crabmeat*

6 *tablespoons grated Swiss* *cheese*
1 *egg*
1 *egg yolk*
⅔ *cup light cream*

Salt and pepper to taste

*Omit sugar

Line 12 small tart pans with the pastry, allowing two per person. Bake at 400° for 5 minutes or until pastry is just set. Sprinkle the bottom of each shell with grated Parmesan. Now divide up the crabmeat among the shells and cover with the grated Swiss cheese. Beat the egg and egg yolk with a fork until just blended, stir in the cream, add salt and pepper. Spoon this custard mixture over the shells until they can hold no more. Bake at 325° for 15 to 20 minutes or until custard is set and golden brown on top. Serve hot.

OYSTERS ON TOAST

For oyster-lovers it is always pleasant to find oysters in a new dress, and this simple but savory presentation will be sure to please.

2 *dozen freshly opened oysters*	2 *teaspoons lemon juice*
3 *tablespoons butter*	½ *teaspoon celery salt*
3 *tablespoons chili sauce*	½ *teaspoon paprika*
3 *teaspoons Worcestershire sauce*	1½ *cups light cream*
	6 *pieces toast*

In a saucepan or chafing dish combine oysters with their liquor, butter, chili sauce, and Worcestershire sauce. Add lemon juice, celery salt, and paprika. Bring to a boil. Cook for 1 minute, stirring constantly. Add the cream and bring to a boil again. Place 4 oysters on each piece of toast and pour the sauce over them. Sprinkle the top with additional paprika.

If you wish to serve these oysters for the main dish at lunch or supper, allow 6 to 8 oysters per person and serve on a bed of puréed spinach.

Pasta

ONE NEED NOT GO to Italy to enjoy real Italian-style pasta. The ingredients for most pasta dishes are obtainable in all American grocery stores, are inexpensive, and the techniques involved in preparing the dishes are simple and foolproof. An unusual pasta dish makes an excellent introduction to a light main course or serves most satisfactorily as a main course at lunch or dinner on crisp fall or winter days. Recipes allow six servings.

GNOCCHI

Although the Italians have many interesting ways of beginning a meal, the most common first course is a pasta dish: spaghetti, ravioli, lasagne, etc. Much as Americans may like these as a main dish, they often find them too heavy to eat as a first course. There are some pasta-type dishes, however, which are not so filling and, I think, more interesting. Gnocchi, in various forms, is an excellent example. Gnocchi serves equally well as the main dish for lunch or supper and is especially good if accompanied by cold ham, chicken, beef, or cold cuts.

Most gnocchi is made from a pâté-à-chou paste, frequently mixed with mashed potatoes as in Gnocchi Parisienne and Gnocchi Piedmont. Gnocchi al Romano, however, is made from a cereal paste and is even simpler to prepare and quite as attractive to serve.

GNOCCHI AL ROMANO

Golden brown circles overlapping in an attractive pattern in the serving dish will inspire the most lagging appetite.

¼ *pound butter*	½ *pound cream of wheat*
4½ *cups milk*	1 *beaten egg*
½ *teaspoon salt*	½ *cup grated Parmesan*
⅛ *teaspoon nutmeg*	*cheese*

Cut the butter into the milk, add salt and nutmeg and bring to the boil. Slowly stir in ½ pound cream of wheat and cook, stirring, until thick. Stir a bit of the mixture into the beaten egg to warm it and then add it to the mixture. Stir in the grated Parmesan. Spread the mixture ½ inch thick on a buttered tray. Cool. Cut into rounds with a biscuit cutter. Roll each round in grated Parmesan cheese and arrange on a shallow buttered ovenproof dish, in concentric circles, the rounds overlapping to form an attractive pattern. Drip melted butter over the surface and brown under the broiler. The whole dish can be made well in advance and kept in the refrigerator, in which case, put into a hot oven for 5 minutes to heat through before browning under broiler.

GNOCCHI PARISIENNE

1 cup water	1½ cups flour
2 tablespoons butter	3 eggs
½ teaspoon salt	¼ cup grated Swiss cheese
¼ teaspoon cayenne	½ teaspoon dry mustard

In a saucepan combine the water, butter, salt, and cayenne. Bring to a rolling boil and add the flour all at once. Stir the mixture constantly until it leaves the side of the pan and forms a ball of dough. Remove the pan from the fire and add the eggs, one at a time, beating well after each addition until all egg has been absorbed. Stir in the grated cheese and mustard. Put the dough into a pastry bag with a large plain tube. Squeeze the dough into long strips into a pan of salted boiling water. Cook over low heat until gnocchi rise to the surface. Remove with a slotted spoon. Cut into pieces about 1 inch long and arrange in a greased shallow baking dish. If you haven't a pastry bag, or don't like working with one, spread the dough on a greased pan or plate and cut into long strips, or grease fingers lightly and shape the dough, then drop it into the boiling water. Make the following sauce to pour over the gnocchi and then brown it under the broiler.

Sauce

2 tablespoons butter	1 cup grated Swiss cheese
3 tablespoons flour	½ teaspoon dry mustard
1 cup milk	1 egg yolk, beaten
½ cup cream	1 tablespoon butter

Melt the butter in a pan, stir in the flour, and when blended to a smooth paste gradually stir in the milk and cook, stirring with a wire whisk, until thickened and smooth. Add the cream and ¼ cup of the cheese and the dry mustard. Mix a little of the sauce with the egg yolk; stir it into the sauce. Pour the sauce over the gnocchi and sprinkle the top with the remaining ¾ cup grated cheese and dot with the butter. Brown under a broiler.

GNOCCHI PIEDMONT

1 *pound potatoes*
¾ *cup flour*
1 *whole egg*

1 *egg yolk*
½ *teaspoon salt*
¼ *teaspoon pepper*

Peel and boil the potatoes until tender, drain, and put them through a ricer. Add the flour, egg and egg yolk, salt and pepper, and beat together until thoroughly blended. Shape into balls the size of a walnut and flatten each ball into a round about ⅓ inch thick. Drop into boiling salted water, or better still, into boiling stock or bouillon. Cook for 10 minutes. Drain and arrange in a greased shallow baking dish. Cover with sauce, either the cheese, as in recipe for Gnocchi Parisienne (see recipe), or a tomato or mushroom sauce. Sprinkle top with cheese and brown under a hot broiler.

CANNELONI

This is another Italian specialty that is very, very special. In the last few years Italian pizza pies and Italian lasagne have become well-known and popular in the States, and I think that very soon canneloni will become equally well-known and popular. It certainly should, for it is a most delicious dish. Each restaurant in Italy seems to have its own version of this dish, but the basic form is always the same: squares of pasta rolled around tasty meat; meat and cheese; or meat, vegetable, and cheese filling arranged in a baking dish and covered with a luscious sauce; sometimes a meat-and-cheese sauce; sometimes a rich cream sauce with cheese overtones; sometimes a tomato-and-cheese sauce; and sometimes a combination of several or all of these. Now you can make your own pasta and cut it into squares to be filled, but this is not necessary to the success of the dish. You can buy the large, in fact gigantic, macaroni for filling. It is usually called manicotti. Making your own pasta might make the dish seem too much trouble and that would be a shame, for although the filling and sauce recipe and directions may take a good deal of space, the carrying out of the directions is really very easy, and if you can buy the pasta ready-made, you will find that you can produce a truly delicious dish with not too much work.

CANNELONI GRAND HOTEL FLORENCE

3 *tablespoons butter*	⅔ *cup white wine*
2 *onions, finely chopped*	2 *tablespoons tomato paste*
1 *small carrot, finely chopped*	1½ *cup meat stock*
1 *stalk celery, finely chopped*	*Salt and pepper to taste*
2 *pounds of lean meat, beef,*	2 *egg yolks*
pork, veal, and chicken in	½ *cup grated Parmesan*
equal parts or in combina-	*cheese*
tion that is convenient	

Parboiled tubes of pasta or squares to be stuffed

In a heavy pot or casserole heat the butter and brown the chopped vegetables. Cut the meat into cubes or smallish pieces and brown lightly on all sides. Pour the white wine, tomato paste, and stock into the pot. Cover tightly and bake for 5 hours at 250°. The meat should be soft and the juices thick.

Pour into a large strainer and collect the juices. Take the meat from the strainer and put through a meat chopper with a fine blade or put into an electric food blender for a few seconds.

Now add to the puréed meat the egg yolks and Parmesan cheese. Mix well and carefully stuff the parboiled pasta. Allow 2 to 3 tubes of pasta for each serving. Arrange the stuffed pasta in a greased shallow baking dish.

Sauce

2 *tablespoons butter or fat*	1 *cup heavy cream or*
2 *tablespoons flour*	*Béchamel Sauce*
½ *cup red wine*	*Parmesan cheese*

Take the butter, or fat that has collected on top of the meat juices, and heat in a saucepan. Stir in flour, and when smooth gradually stir in the reserved meat juices and red wine. Cook, stirring, until thickened and smooth. Pour this sauce over the canneloni. Now pour heavy cream or Béchamel Sauce (see recipe) over the dish and sprinkle the top generously with Parmesan cheese. Put into a 375° oven for 15 minutes.

The whole dish can be made well in advance and stored in the refrigerator or in the freezer. If the dish is cold it will, of course, need additional time in the oven.

A pleasant variation on this dish is a cup of cooked chopped spinach added to the filling.

CANNELONI ROMANO

Meat sauce, as in preceding recipe	3 *tablespoons grated Parmesan*
2 *tablespoons butter*	½ *pound ricotta cheese*
2 *tablespoons flour*	½ *cup finely diced mozzarella*
1½ *cups hot milk*	
2 *egg yolks*	½ *cup chopped ham*
Parboiled pasta for stuffing	

Make the meat sauce as in the preceding recipe. Do not separate the meat from the juices, but put the whole into the blender to make a smooth meaty sauce. Now make a thick cream sauce by melting the butter and blending in the flour, then gradually stirring in the hot milk. Cook this, stirring, until it is thick and smooth. Allow it to cool, add the egg yolks, Parmesan, ricotta, and mozzarella cheeses, the ham, and ¾ cup of the meat sauce.

Carefully stuff the pasta with this mixture and arrange them in a shallow baking dish that has the bottom covered with a thin layer of the meat sauce. If there is any of the stuffing left over, spoon it on top of the canneloni, then put a tablespoon of reserved meat sauce or tomato sauce on each, sprinkle the top with Parmesan and bake at 400° for 10 minutes.

This dish can be made in advance and stored in the refrigerator or freezer. If it is cold when it goes into the oven, it will need additional time to become thoroughly heated. And it must be hot and bubbly when brought to the table.

SPAGHETTI À LA NAPOLITAINE

Spaghetti as a first course seems rather heavy to Americans who usually eat it as a main course. However, if served with a meatless sauce and followed by a main course unaccompanied by a starch, it goes to make up a fine menu, as those of you who have eaten in Italy know. This spaghetti dish is also a very good complement to a sauceless meat course, especially roast veal or chicken or sautéed veal cutlet. I acquired this recipe in Italy, and I find it so much better than any found here that I cannot resist giving it to you.

4 tablespoons butter
1 large onion, finely chopped
2 tablespoons flour
1 pound red ripe tomatoes
2 tablespoons tomato paste
1 bay leaf
Large sprig parsley
2 cloves garlic, crushed

½ cup bouillon
1 teaspoon salt
¼ teaspoon pepper
1 tablespoon sugar
⅔ pound spaghetti
2 tablespoons olive oil
Parmesan cheese to sprinkle on top

Melt 2 tablespoons of butter in a pan, add onion, cover and simmer to soften slightly. Add the flour, stir well and draw off the fire. Cut the tomatoes in four and scoop out the pips. Do this above a strainer, catching the juice to add to the pan. Add the tomatoes, juice, tomato paste, herbs, crushed garlic, bouillon and seasoning to the pan. Simmer to a pulp. Rub through a strainer, return to pan and reduce the sauce until thick. Adjust seasoning to taste. This may be made well in advance and reheated. It freezes well.

Boil the spaghetti in plenty of boiling salted water with a tablespoon of oil. When just tender, drain and rinse in hot water. Now melt the remaining butter and the olive oil in the pan; when they begin to bubble put back the spaghetti and toss lightly until all the strands are coated. Serve at once with the Neapolitan sauce and a generous sprinkling of Parmesan.

Molded Dishes

A COOL, COLORFUL MOLD is a delightful thought for beginning a dinner on a hot summer day, or as the mainstay for lunch or supper. It will leave you refreshed, not weighed down. And molds can be so attractive that even the most jaded appetite will be whetted. The following recipes yield six servings.

COLD SMOKED HADDOCK MOUSSE

This attractive fish mousse can be made with any white-meat fish, but a smoked fish makes it tastier and more unusual.

1 pound smoked haddock, cooked, skinned and flaked (simmer the haddock in a cup of milk until tender)
1 tablespoon gelatin
1 cup Aspic Jelly (recipe below)

1 cup mayonnaise
1 cup heavy cream, partially whipped
2 hard-cooked eggs
Remainder of Aspic Jelly to garnish

Have the fish cooked and cold. Soften the gelatin in the aspic, then dissolve over hot water. Combine the aspic and gelatin with the mayonnaise and whipped cream, and then fold in the flaked fish. Turn into a soufflé dish to ¾ full. Leave to set, then decorate the top with sliced hard-cooked eggs. Fill to the top with aspic jelly just on the point of setting.

ASPIC JELLY

1¾ pints good well-flavored Fish Stock (see recipe)	¼ cup sherry
	2 tablespoons gelatin
½ cup white wine	2 tablespoons vinegar
2 egg whites	

Put the cold stock, wine, sherry, gelatin and vinegar into a pan over gentle heat. When warm add the egg whites whipped to a froth, and whisk until the boiling point is reached. Allow the mixture to boil, without stirring, to the top of the pan, draw aside, and boil up twice more. Allow to settle five minutes and then strain.

Allow the mousse to set for several hours or overnight. Unmold unto a serving platter and garnish with sprigs of watercress or parsley.

FISH IN ASPIC

2 pounds firm fish (red mullet or snapper is ideal, but if not obtainable, use flounder or halibut)	2 carrots, sliced
	2 stalks celery, chopped
	3 sprigs parsley, chopped
	1 teaspoon salt
4 cups water	4 eggs
1 large onion, sliced	4 lemons, juiced

Have the fish market clean fish, cut off fins and remove eyes, but not head. Cut fish into thick, 1½-inch slices.

Boil together the water and chopped vegetables and seasoning for 20 minutes. Add the fish and simmer for 20 minutes or until fish is tender. Remove fish from stock; skin, and bone it carefully, putting skin and bones back into the stock. Continue to cook stock until it has reduced to 2 cups. Then strain the stock through a fine strainer and cheesecloth.

In a mixing bowl beat the eggs until well-blended, add the juice of the 4 lemons slowly, stirring constantly so as not to curdle. Add the clear stock, check seasoning, add the fish broken into chunks. You want as many good-sized ½-inch- to 1-inch-square pieces as possible. Pour into an oiled fish mold. Let stand for at least 4 hours, unmold on a serving platter. Serve garnished with parsley and accompanied by a bowl of mayonnaise.

Homemade mayonnaise is undoubtedly better than commercial mayonnaise, so if you have an extra few minutes, try the recipe given below.

MAYONNAISE

This simple recipe makes an excellent mayonnaise. It is so much better than the commercial kind that once you have tried it I think you will become a convert to the homemade variety.

1 *cup salad oil*	Salt and pepper to taste
1 *whole egg*	Dash cayenne
⅛ *teaspoon dry mustard*	Juice of 1 lemon, strained

Put ¼ cup of the oil in an electric blender with the egg, seasoning, and lemon juice. Run at low speed until well-blended; continue to run at low speed while gradually pouring in the remainder of the oil. Run until thick. If it does not get as thick as you like it, run at high speed for a few seconds. If by some remote chance it should separate, add another egg and run until blended and smooth. Taste, and if not tart enough, add a few more drops of lemon juice.

AVOCADO RING

1 envelope gelatin	2 tablespoons lime juice (if
¼ cup water	no limes are available, add
1 cup mashed avocado pulp	1 tablespoon additional
½ cup mayonnaise	lemon juice)
3 tablespoons lemon juice	1 teaspoon salt
1 cup heavy cream, whipped	

Soften the gelatin in the water in a small metal bowl or cup, and then place in a pan of hot water over a low flame until the gelatin is completely dissolved. Combine the avocado pulp, mayonnaise, lemon juice, lime juice, and salt. Stir in the dissolved gelatin and fold in the whipped cream. Pour the mixture into a ring mold and chill for at least four hours. It must be completely firm. Unmold the ring onto a serving dish, fill the center with cold boiled lobster meat, or cold boiled shrimp, or with any seafood salad. Garnish with sprigs of watercress and accompany with a bowl of mayonnaise. The ring is good by itself and need not be filled at all. However, if used for the main course at lunch or supper, it would not be substantial enough unless filled. Chicken or turkey salad also makes a good filling.

EGG MOLD SALAD

This salad is attractive, different, and delicious.

2 *tablespoons or envelopes gelatin*	⅔ *cup chowchow*
	⅔ *cup chopped parsley*
½ *cup water*	2 *tablespoons Worcestershire sauce*
10 *hard-boiled eggs*	
⅔ *cup chopped ripe olives*	1 *teaspoon salt*

1 *cup mayonnaise*

Soften the gelatin in the water and then dissolve it over hot water; place a small bowl with the gelatin in a pan of hot water over a low flame until gelatin is completely dissolved. Put the hard-boiled eggs through a ricer or rub them through a colander. Mix the eggs with the olives, chowchow, parsley, Worcestershire sauce, salt, and mayonnaise. Stir in the dissolved gelatin. When all is well-mixed, pour into a large mold or into individual molds. Chill for at least 4 hours or until firm. Cover a platter or individual serving plate with finely shredded lettuce and unmold the egg salad onto this. Accompany with a bowl of mayonnaise (see recipe). If you are feeling extravagant, top the mold with caviar.

CREAM CHEESE AND TOMATO ASPIC

Here is an easy, inexpensive, and pretty dish to make.

2 *tablespoons gelatin*	2 *tablespoons grated onion*
½ *cup water*	1 *teaspoon Worcestershire*
1 *can condensed tomato soup*	½ *cup finely diced celery*
	1 *cup mayonnaise*
9 *ounces cream cheese*	*Watercress for garnish*

Soften the gelatin in the water. Heat the soup, add the gelatin and stir until completely dissolved. Have the cream cheese at room temperature, work with a fork until softened and beat it into the hot soup. Add the grated onion, Worcestershire sauce, celery, and mayonnaise. Pour into a ring mold. Chill for at least 4 hours. Unmold on a bed of shredded lettuce and garnish with watercress. If serving for lunch, fill the center with cold boiled shrimp and pass a bowl of mayonnaise.

COLD CHICKEN MOUSSE

1½ tablespoons gelatin
¼ cup cold water
2 cups firmly packed cooked chicken
2 cups chicken stock
1 cup milk
3 egg yolks, slightly beaten

1 tablespoon grated onion
Pinch thyme
2 tablespoons chili sauce
1 tablespoon horseradish sauce
Salt and pepper to taste
1 cup heavy cream, whipped

Soften the gelatin in the cold water. Place the chicken, 1 cup of the stock, and the milk in a blender and run until mixture is very smooth. Add the remaining cup of stock to the egg yolks, cook, stirring constantly, over low heat until slightly thickened. Add the gelatin and stir until completely dissolved. Now combine all the ingredients except the whipped cream and chill until it is just beginning to set. Fold in the whipped cream and turn into a 2-quart mold. Chill for at least 4 hours. Unmold, and garnish with slices of tomato and mayonnaise.

SALMON MOLD WITH CUCUMBER DRESSING

1 envelope or tablespoon gelatin
¼ cup cold water
1 teaspoon salt
1 teaspoon dry mustard
Dash cayenne
2 tablespoons flour

2 tablespoons sugar
2 egg yolks
1 cup milk
3 tablespoons vinegar
1½ tablespoons butter
2 cups flaked canned red salmon

1 large cucumber, peeled and chopped fine

Soften the gelatin in the cold water. Mix the dry ingredients in a saucepan, add the egg yolks, and mix well. Add the milk and, continuing to stir gradually, add the vinegar. Cook over a low heat, stirring constantly until thickened. Add the gelatin and stir until dissolved. Add the butter, and stir until melted. Fold in the salmon and turn into six individual molds or one large mold. Chill until firm, or at least 4 hours. Unmold on a bed of lettuce and serve with mayonnaise (see recipe) or sour cream to which the chopped cucumber has been added.

Out-of-Hand First Courses

OUT-OF-HAND first courses are good any time of year, but particularly nice in summer for they are easy to get together and are usually cool. Recipes serve six.

MELON AND PROSCIUTTO HAM

Here is a delicious combination and one that refreshes without filling. Arrange three 1-inch wedges of melon—honeydew, casaba, or cantalope are equally good—on each plate alternately with 3 thin slices of Prosciutto ham. Be certain the melon is cold.

RED CAVIAR, SOUR CREAM, AND WATERCRESS

Put a mound of red caviar, a mound of sour cream, and a large sprig of fresh watercress on each plate with 3 very thin triangles of pumpernickel bread. Have additional pumpernickel to pass.

SEAFOOD COCKTAILS

Cold cooked shrimp, lobster, or crabmeat—or a combination of these—arranged in a sherbert dish lined with lettuce leaves and topped with a Cocktail Sauce, Rémoulade Sauce, or Ravigote Sauce (recipes follow) is a popular and good way to begin a meal.

•

COCKTAIL SAUCE

¾ cup chili sauce
1 tablespoon drained horseradish
2 teaspoons lemon juice
½ teaspoon Worcestershire sauce
Salt and pepper to taste
Dash cayenne

Combine all the ingredients and mix well. Chill thoroughly before using. Keeps for weeks in a refrigerator.

RÉMOULADE SAUCE

This is especially good with shrimp.

1½ cups Mayonnaise (see recipe)
1 teaspoon prepared mustard
1 tablespoon finely chopped sweet gherkin
1 teaspoon finely chopped capers
1 teaspoon chopped parsley
1 teaspoon chopped chervil
⅓ teaspoon chopped tarragon
½ teaspoon anchovy paste

Press the chopped gherkin and capers in a cloth to extract excess liquid. Mix all the ingredients together thoroughly. Serve cold.

RAVIGOTE SAUCE

This is especially good with crabmeat.

3 hard-cooked egg yolks forced through a sieve or ricer
2 fresh egg yolks
⅛ teaspoon each paprika, dry mustard, and sugar
1 teaspoon each finely minced onion, shallot, parsley, and chives
Salt and pepper to taste
⅔ cup Mayonnaise (see recipe)

Beat the fresh egg yolks; then beat in the sieved yolks and the seasoning and herbs. When well-blended, fold in the Mayonnaise. Serve cold.

AVOCADO WITH SEAFOOD

A lovely and delicious variation of the seafood cocktail is avocado with seafood: avocado halves heaped high with a mixture of seafood and avocado meat, bound together with Russian dressing.

3 medium-sized avocados, ripe but not soft
⅔ cup cold cooked shrimp
⅔ cup cold cooked lobster cut into bite-sized pieces
½ cup cold cooked crab
Salt and pepper to taste
Russian dressing
Paprika

Cut the avocados in half and carefully scoop out the meat. Place the seafood in a bowl, season to taste, cut the avocado into large dice and add to the seafood. Pour on just enough dressing to bind and toss all lightly, being careful not to mash the avocado. Pile the mixture into the avocado shells, sprinkle the top with paprika. Place each half on a lettuce leaf on individual serving plates.

OYSTERS OR CLAMS ON THE HALF SHELL

Six to ten raw oysters or clams on the half shell arranged in a circle on each plate, with a small bowl of cocktail sauce in the middle and a wedge of lemon on the side, is an excellent way to get a meal off to a good start. You have only to buy really fresh oysters or clams, scrub them well, open with a sharp knife, and discard the top shell. Chill well before serving. For the sauce you can use the Cocktail Sauce (see recipe) or just mix ketchup and lemon juice to suit your taste.

Vol-au-Vent

THE VOL-AU-VENT, a shell of flakey tender puff paste, in France called a *mille-feuille*, filled with any one of a number of delightful creamy items—chicken, chicken livers, seafood, sweetbreads, mushrooms, brains, kidneys, or ham—is a beautiful and delicious way to start a dinner and the finest answer to "what to serve?" at an important lunch. The fillings for vol-au-vent are as varied as your imagination allows, but the shell is constant, so we will begin with that. Recipes for puff paste always sound complicated, but are in reality quite simple: they are much more difficult to describe than to make. Recipes yield six servings.

PUFF PASTE

2 cups flour
½ teaspoon salt
½ to ¾ cup ice water
½ pound sweet butter, well-washed (that is, kneaded and squeezed in your hands in a bowl of ice water or under icy cold running water until malleable; butter must be pliable and waxy, but not soft or creamy)

Sift the flour and salt in a mound on a pastry board or working counter. Make a well in the center of the flour. Pour 2 tablespoons of ice water into the hollow and gradually work in the flour with the fingers and heel of one hand. Continue adding a little water and working in the flour until the dough barely holds together. Be careful not to work the dough. The dough at this point must not have any elasticity but must have just enough moisture to hold together and to permit rolling it out. Collect all the dough on the board with a scraper and roll it into a ball. Reflour the board lightly and roll out the dough into a rectangle about ¼ inch thick. In the center third of the dough place the cake of washed butter which has been chilling in the refrigerator while you prepared the dough. Fold one third of the dough over the butter, then fold the remaining third on top of this. Fold in the ends. Roll this rectangle out lengthwise and fold it in thirds again. Turn the dough so that one of the open ends faces front. This is called a turn. Roll out and fold in thirds again; this constitutes two turns. Wrap the dough in waxed paper and chill in the refrigerator for at least 1 hour. You may leave it for several hours or overnight. Repeat this operation two more times, chilling for at least ½ hour in between. After the last chilling, roll out the dough into the desired shape. You can shape it into one large shell to be filled, then cut and served at the table, or you can shape it into individual shells to be filled and served on individual serving plates. If you desire a large shell, roll out the dough ⅝ inch thick, cut out a circle 8 to 10 inches in diameter, then press ¾ way through the dough a 6- to 8-inch inner circle, leaving a rim of 1 inch. Be careful not to cut all the way through or you will have a loose rim with no bottom. Place the circle on a cookie sheet that you have moistened with cold water. As the dough bakes, the inner circle will rise up, and when baked, gently lift out the inner circle, saving it to use as a cover should you want one, or you can use it for another purpose later, possibly as a basis for a dessert. Pull out excess dough if necessary to make a hollow shell. After shaping the dough you can, if you wish, make a decorative edging by scoring the outside of the shell with a knife. Chill the shaped dough for at least 15 minutes before baking. It must be ice cold when it goes into the hot oven. Bake at 450° for 10 minutes, or until well-puffed and golden. Reduce heat to 375° and bake 25 minutes longer.

For individual shells follow the same procedure but roll out dough ¼ inch thick and cut small circles of desired size. When pressing out the inner circle, leave a rim of only ⅓ inch. Bake at 450° for 10 minutes. Reduce heat to 375° and bake 10 minutes longer.

FILLINGS FOR VOL-AU-VENT

The fillings for the puff paste shells are almost numberless. You can start with fresh materials or use the vol-au-vent as a means of presenting leftovers, whether they are chicken, meat, fish, or vegetables. You need only make a Béchamel or Mornay Sauce (see recipes) to bind the leftovers together and you have an elegant dish. Any one of the fillings used for Crêpes (see recipes) or for Coquilles (see recipes) could be equally well-presented in a vol-au-vent. I will give only three recipes for fillings here. In each case you will see how easy it would be to substitute other meats, or seafood, or vegetables for the one the recipe calls for. The shells and filling can both be made ahead of time; just reheat the filling thoroughly before putting in the shells, and if the shells have become limp, recrisp by putting them in a hot oven for 2 or 3 minutes.

CHICKEN AND HAM VOL-AU-VENT

2 tablespoons butter
3 tablespoons flour
1½ cups Chicken Stock (bouillon cubes or chicken concentrate may be used to make this if you have no stock on hand)
2 egg yolks
¾ cup heavy cream
Salt to taste

Dash cayenne
¼ cup sherry
2 cups cooked chicken meat, diced (turkey may be used)
1 cup cooked ham, diced (this may be omitted and an extra cup of chicken meat used)
½ pound mushrooms, sliced and sautéed in butter until tender

Melt the butter in a saucepan, blend in the flour and cook the roux until it is golden. Stir in the chicken stock and continue to cook, stirring until it thickens. Beat the yolks slightly, then mix them with the cream. Add a bit of the hot mixture to the eggs and cream, then slowly stir it into the sauce. Season to taste with salt and cayenne. Do not permit the sauce to boil after the addition of the eggs. Cook only until thickened, stirring constantly. Stir in the sherry, chicken, ham, and mushrooms. Continue to cook until heated thoroughly. Fill the vol-au-vent shell with the mixture. If you wish to give the dish an added touch, garnish the top of the vol-au-vent with a lattice work of ham cut into long narrow strips and arrange slices of sautéed mushrooms in the openings of the lattice work.

SEAFOOD VOL-AU-VENT

2 pounds seafood—1 pound scallops and 1 pound shrimp, shelled and deveined, or use only ½ pound scallops and shrimp and ½ each of sole and lobster. (The type and proportion of seafood may be varied to suit your taste, your purse, and your convenience. If you use mussels, clams, or oysters, reserve their liquor and add it to the sauce.)

2 cups white wine
2 tablespoons butter
1 tablespoon minced onion
2 tablespoons flour
2 egg yolks
½ cup heavy cream
Salt and pepper to taste
½ pound mushrooms, sliced and cooked in water to cover with a few drops of lemon juice for 5 minutes (this is optional)

Simmer the seafood in 2 cups white wine for 5 minutes. If using lobster and sole, cut it into large dices before cooking. Drain and reserve the liquid. Slice the scallops. In a saucepan melt the butter, sauté the minced onion until tender, stir in the flour and cook the roux until it is smooth and golden. Stir in the liquid reserved from cooking the seafood and the liquid from the mushrooms, and cook, stirring, until it thickens. Combine the slightly beaten egg yolks and cream, add a little of the hot sauce, bit by bit to warm it, and then stir the egg mixture back into the sauce and continue to cook, stirring, until thickened. Do not permit it to boil. Add the seafood and mushrooms and heat thoroughly. Turn the mixture into a large vol-au-vent shell or into individual shells and serve.

SWEETBREADS VOL-AU-VENT

Sweetbreads are a natural for vol-au-vent, especially in company with mushrooms. There are many sauces that go well with this combination. The sauce used in the Chicken and Ham Vol-au-Vent (see recipes) is excellent. A béchamel sauce is good. The simple cream and brandy sauce given below is designed to bring out the best in both the sweetbreads and the pastry.

2 *pairs sweetbreads, par-boiled and chilled*	*Salt and pepper*
	⅛ *teaspoon nutmeg*
Flour for dredging	1 *pound mushrooms, sliced*
4 *tablespoons butter*	½ *cup sherry*
2 *tablespoons warm brandy*	1 *tablespoon lemon juice*

1½ *cups heavy cream*

Slice the parboiled and chilled sweetbreads and dredge lightly with flour. Sauté the slices in butter until golden brown. Pour the warm brandy over them and set aflame. When the flame has burned out, season the sweetbreads with salt, pepper, and nutmeg. Add the sliced mushrooms, cover and simmer for 4 minutes. Stir in the sherry and simmer for another 4 minutes. Gradually add the lemon juice and cream. Heat through but do not allow it to boil. Fill the vol-au-vent shells with the mixture and serve. If sauce is too thin, thicken with a little cornstarch dissolved in cold water.

Combination Cheese Dishes

CHEESE IS A whole and wholesome food. Good as it is by itself, its chief merit for the cook is its ability to blend with and improve so many other foods. It goes well with pastry, with vegetables, fish, fowl, or meat. The following recipes demonstrate a few unusual and delicious methods of using cheese to get a dinner off to a good start or to make a memorable lunch. Recipes yield six servings.

QUICHE LORRAINE

The quiche, long a French favorite, has become quite popular here in the past few years, and any list of suggestions for first courses or luncheon and supper dishes would be woefully inadequate without a high recommendation of the tasty onion, cheese, ham, and custard pie as a way to start a dinner or to lunch or sup.

1 9-inch pie shell, partially baked
3 slices baked ham or equivalent amount of crisp bacon
2 large onions, sliced fine
2 tablespoons butter
½ pound Swiss cheese, cut into strips
2 cups milk, heated
4 eggs
Salt and pepper
Dash nutmeg

Cut the ham into bite-size pieces and scatter them over the partially baked Pie Crust (see recipe). Sauté the sliced onions in butter until tender but not brown. Spread them over the ham. Cover with the Swiss cheese. Heat milk until skin forms on top. Now make a custard by beating the eggs with a dash of salt, pepper, and nutmeg, and gradually blend in the warm milk. Continue to stir the mixture constantly over low heat until the custard begins to thicken. Pour it over the ham, onions, and cheese in the pie shell. Bake the quiche at 375° for 45 minutes or until the custard is set and golden on top. Serve piping hot, directly from the pan.

The ham, onions, and cheese may be arranged in the pie shell and the custard cooked long in advance, thus leaving only the combining and baking for the last minute.

LOBSTER OR SEAFOOD QUICHE

Not so well-known as Quiche Lorraine, but equally good, if you like seafood, is Seafood Quiche.

Follow directions for Quiche Lorraine, in the preceding recipe, substituting lobster, shrimp, or crab, or a combination of these, for the ham.

ALSATIAN ONION TART

This is a Quiche Lorraine without the ham or bacon and with twice the amount of onions, so follow directions on page 89, omitting the ham and using 4 onions instead of 2.

PIE CRUST

As there are several recipes in this book, both in the sections on desserts (THE END) and on first courses (THE BEGINNING), that require pie crusts, I shall give here the directions for making pie crust usable in all recipes calling for it.

The shortening should be as cold as possible. The water should be iced.

Use a pastry cloth and rolling-pin cover and a pastry blender.

Most important of all, use a light hand. The dough should be handled as lightly and as little as possible. Do not be disturbed if you are unable to pick up your crust in one piece. You can press the edges of the pieces together in the pan, and after it is baked the patches will not show. A crust that is smooth and easy to handle is likely to be tough.

For 1 two-crust pie or 2 single-crust pies:

1½ cups sifted all-purpose flour
1 teaspoon salt
½ cup plus 1 tablespoon high-grade vegetable shortening
3 tablespoons iced water

Sift the flour and salt into a mixing bowl. Cut in one half of the shortening with a pastry blender until it is well incorporated. (This makes for tenderness.) Now cut in the remaining shortening only until it is the size of large peas. (This gives the crust its flakiness.) Sprinkle the flour mixture with the iced water and mix ever so slightly. Gather up half of the dough with your hand and form it into a loose ball. Place the ball in the middle of a well-floured pastry cloth. Rub flour well onto the rolling pin and roll out the dough into a circle approximately ⅛ inch thick. Do not attempt to turn the crust over and roll it on the other side. Slide a spatula under the crust to loosen it from the cloth. Fold it in half, lift it up gently, lay it folded across the center of a 9-inch pie plate, and then unfold it.

For a prebaked crust, bake 15 to 20 minutes at 400°. Check once or twice during baking because you will want a light golden crust, not a dark brown one.

If the pie is to be filled before baking, place the crust in a hot oven, 425°, for 5 minutes, or until slightly glazed. Then fill and put on the top crust. Make 2 or 3 gashes in it to allow steam to escape. Return to a 350° to 375° oven and bake until done.

SPANAKOPITTA
(GREEK SPINACH-CHEESE PIE)

The Greeks and Turks have a crisp and tasty way to start a meal: layers of paper-thin crispy pastry alternating with a tasty spinach and cheese, or just cheese, filling. The Greeks call the pastry *filos* and the Turks call it *borek*. It is seldom made in the home but bought by the pound from bake shops. It can be purchased here in most Greek or other Middle Eastern delicatessens or in specialty food departments in the stores in large cities. If *filos* or *borek* is unobtainable, ask for the packaged strudel sheets. It is essentially the same and more frequently handled by American shops. All Hungarian food shops carry the packaged strudel sheets. This pastry is snow white and as thin as onion skin paper; in fact, when piled up it looks like a ream of typing paper. If well-wrapped it keeps for weeks in the refrigerator, or it can be frozen for an indefinite period. It must not be allowed to stand out in the air, for it dries out quickly and cracks when handled.

20 8- by 10-inch-square
    sheets of filos or strudel
    dough
½ pound spinach
1 medium onion, finely
    chopped and sautéed in
    butter until tender
3 eggs beaten
⅓ pound Feta cheese crum-
    bled (this is a Greek
    cheese; if unobtainable
    use cottage cheese and 3
    tablespoons Parmesan
    cheese)
1 tablespoon chopped parsley
    (optional)
1 tablespoon olive oil
Salt and pepper to taste
⅓ to ½ pound melted but-
    ter to brush on pastry

Wash spinach, chop coarsely, and cook until just barely tender, or about 2 minutes; drain thoroughly. Mix the sautéed onion, eggs, cheese, parsley, and olive oil. Stir in the spinach. Season to taste. Butter a square baking dish, approximately 10 by 10 by 2. Cut the sheets of pastry to fit the dish. Place a square of pastry in the baking dish, brush it with melted butter, place another sheet in dish, again brush with butter, and repeat until you have stacked 10 sheets of pastry, each one well-brushed with melted butter. Now spread the spinach and cheese mixture over the pastry and then cover with the remaining 10 sheets, putting down one at a time and brushing it generously with butter. With a sharp knife cut the pie on the diagonal into diamond shaped wedges. Bake at 350° for 1 hour or until puffy and brown.

GREEK CHEESE PIE

Omit the spinach and parsley and proceed as for Spinach-Cheese Pie in preceding recipe.

PAPUTSAKIS
(LITTLE SHOES)

The Greeks have another delicious way to start a meal: zucchini stuffed with a cheese sauce, which they call *paputsakis,* meaning little shoes.

6 *medium-sized zucchini*	*Greek cheese Feta (if this*
2 *tablespoons butter*	*is unobtainable use Swiss*
3 *tablespoons flour*	*cheese or a sharp cheddar)*
1½ *cups warm milk*	2 *egg yolks mixed with*
1 *cup grated or crumbled*	¼ *cup light cream or milk*
cheese, preferably the	1 *cup diced ham (optional)*

Cut the zucchini in half, lengthwise. Cover with boiling salted water and cook until barely tender, or about 5 minutes. Drain. When cool enough to handle, scoop out the seeded core.

Melt the butter in a saucepan. Stir in the flour, and when blended, gradually stir in the warm milk. Cook over low heat stirring constantly until thickened and smooth. Stir in the grated cheese, and when melted, carefully stir in the slightly beaten egg yolks mixed with the cream or milk. Do not boil after the addition of the egg yolks.

If you have a little leftover ham on hand, dice it and fold it into the sauce. Now spoon this thick cheese sauce in the hollowed-out zucchini. Arrange in a flat baking dish and bake at 375° for 20 minutes. Serve piping hot. The whole dish may be made well in advance and stored in the refrigerator. In this case it will need an additional 10 minutes in the oven.

SWISS CHEESE FONDUE

The Swiss serve fondue for a first course, but I think most Americans find it rather rich for that purpose. However, it is such a useful item to have in your cooking repertoire for impromptu supper or late evening snacks that I am including an excellent recipe for fondue here. The fondue is eaten from a common pot, everyone dipping his hunk of bread into the fondue, creating an atmosphere of good humor and gaiety.

2 *cloves garlic*	*Dash nutmeg*
1½ *pounds Swiss cheese*	*Freshly ground black pepper*
2 *tablespoons butter*	⅛ *teaspoon soda*
2 *cups dry white wine*	*Large loaf French bread cut*
4 *teaspoons cornstarch*	*into inch-square hunks*
¼ *cup* kirschwasser	

Rub an earthenware casserole or chafing dish with the cloves of garlic which should then be crushed and left in the bottom of the casserole. Put the cheese, butter, and white wine in the casserole, and place on a moderate heat and stir with a wooden spoon until cheese is creamy and barely simmering. If the cheese forms into a thick mass, continue to stir, and it will be reabsorbed. Dissolve the cornstarch in the *kirschwasser* and stir this into the mixture. Continue to cook, stirring until mixture bubbles, season with salt and pepper and a dash of nutmeg. Fold in the soda at the last minute. This makes the fondue lighter.

Place the casserole on a spirit lamp or on the small flame of a chafing set. The flame must be just high enough to keep the fondue cooking ever so gently during the meal.

Each participant in the fondue-eating must spear hunks of bread on a fork and dip into the fondue, turning it until the bread is well coated, and . . . good appetite!

FRIED CHEESE SQUARES

I first ran across this delicious way to start a meal in Quebec, where it was listed on the menu as Fondue Parme-

san. I was surprised when it appeared, for it bore no re-
semblance to a fondue as I knew it. I was served three
golden brown squares. When cut into, they oozed cheesey
goodness, but did not run on the plate.

The mixture must be made a day or more in advance,
leaving only the deep-fat frying to the last minute.

4 *tablespoons butter or* *margarine*	1 *bay leaf*
1 *onion, minced*	1 *tablespoon cornstarch*
½ *cup flour*	1 *cup grated Swiss cheese*
1 *quart hot milk*	½ *cup Parmesan cheese*
¼ *teaspoon salt*	3 *egg yolks*
Pinch thyme	*Fine dry bread crumbs*
	2 *beaten eggs*

Melt the butter in top part of double boiler, add the
minced onion and cook until tender, but do not allow to
brown. Stir in the flour and when well-blended, gradually
stir in the hot milk. Add salt and herbs. Whisk until
smooth. Now put over the bottom part of the double
boiler and cook over the hot water for one hour. Rub
through a fine sieve. Return to pan and stir in the cornstarch that you have dissolved in a little cold milk. Cook
for 1 minute. The mixture must be very very thick. Stir in
the grated cheeses. Beat the egg yolks with a fork and
carefully add them to the hot mixture; warm the yolks
with a little of the hot mixture before stirring them into the
pan. Grease a 9-inch-square cake pan and spread out the
mixture. Put into the refrigerator to chill. When cold and
set, cut into squares, roll each square in fine crumbs, then
dip in beaten egg and roll again in the crumbs until evenly
coated. Set in refrigerator until ready to fry. Fry in hot
deep fat until golden brown. Fry only three or four at one
time and keep warm in the oven until they are all ready.

THE END

Any one course can make or break a meal, for a meal must be regarded as a whole. A course or dish may be good in itself, but if it is part of a bad meal, the enjoyment of it is lost. Each dish should be planned in the context of the entire meal. This is no more true of the dessert than of the other courses. However, the dessert, being the climax, is perhaps the most noticed part of the meal. It is like the hat that completes the well-dressed woman's ensemble. It can be the glamorous hat that accents the basic black dress, or it can be a simple whiff of veiling that makes the elaborate dress seem just right. The dessert must leave the diner satisfied but not stuffed. It must carry a large part of the responsibility for making the whole meal a pleasant memory.

A basic rule is that there is no dessert that is always good. Your favorite may be one that is good in itself, that is, when considered alone. But it may be a poor ending to many a meal. The best dessert depends on the other courses and on the season and the climate. Your family or guests will not appreciate a rich date and nut torte or a gooey pecan pie on a hot summer evening or after a heavy main course. Similarly, you would not want to serve a dessert heavy in cream after a main dish with a rich cream sauce.

When spring comes and the first warm days make one feel light and summery, people are as tired of the heavier desserts as they are of their winter clothing. Enough, then, of chocolate, nuts, and rich pastry. The time has come for fresh fruits, light Bavarian and Spanish creams garnished with berries, or gelatin fruit molds, and angel foods or meringues with fresh berries and fruit, or bombes and ice cream molds served with diced fruit and melon balls. When summer draws to a close and one feels surfeited with fresh fruit and berries, it's time to bring on the baked fruit pies, tortes, and tarts. A bit later the pumpkin pies, baked custards, and crêmes will be most appreciated. Finally, you are again ravenously hungry for chocolate desserts and gooey nut concoctions.

This section is by no means an encyclopedia of desserts. Rather, it is a selection of 65 delightful ways to end a meal: few enough to be included in the working inventory of any cook who cares about good food; large enough to provide a fitting end to almost any meal in any season.

These recipes yield six servings.

Cakes and Tortes

MANY HAVE TO VISIT FRANCE before realizing what an elegant dessert a cake can make. One need not scorn the loaf cake and substantial layer cake so loved by hungry families to appreciate that a book devoted to "elegant recipes" must include a few for unusual cakes that fit that description. Once you have ended a meal triumphantly with a dessert cake, you will be on the lookout for other dessert-cake ideas. A torte is a type of cake; it differs from the usual cake in that eggs are the leavening agent, and ground nuts, cracker or bread crumbs are used for the body instead of flour.

WHIPPED CREAM CAKE WITH FRESH COCONUT ICING

This is a delicate creamy-textured cake that makes a superb dessert when filled and frosted with whipped cream into which has been folded fresh grated coconut. It is such a luscious cake that almost any of your favorite icings would go well with it. Whipped cream, into which you have mixed fresh fruit or berries or grated sweet chocolate, is very good, but fresh coconut is so delicious that you will surely want to use it unless it is unavailable. The batter must be put together by hand for it is too delicate to risk overbeating with an electric beater.

1 *cup whipping cream*	1 *teaspoon vanilla*
1 *cup sugar*	1½ *cups cake flour*
2 *eggs, beaten*	2 *teaspoons baking powder*
½ *teaspoon salt*	

Whip the cream until slightly thick, that is, when it just begins to hold shape; fold in the sugar, beaten eggs, and vanilla. Sift and then measure the flour. Add the baking powder and salt to the flour and sift over the cream mixture. Mix together only until smooth. Pour the batter into 2 eight-inch greased layer pans. Bake at 375° for 25 minutes. Allow cakes to cool in the pans; then remove to a serving plate, fill and frost.

Icing

1 *cup whipping cream*	*Vanilla*
Sugar	1 *cup fresh coconut, grated*

To make the fresh coconut icing, whip until stiff the cup of heavy cream, flavor it to taste with sugar and vanilla, and then mix in the cup of fresh grated coconut.

ORANGE CREAM TORTE

This is a moist, airy cake, a type of sponge cake, perfumed with orange and moistened with just enough orange juice to pleasantly surprise and perplex the uninitiated.

Combine and beat until thick

5 egg yolks
½ cup sugar
2 tablespoons orange juice

1 teaspoon grated orange rind
½ teaspoon lemon extract or 1 tablespoon lemon juice

Beat until frothy

5 egg whites   ½ teaspoon salt

Add and beat until rounded peaks are formed

½ cup sugar

Spread the egg yolk mixture over the beaten egg whites and carefully fold together.

Sift and then measure

1 cup cake flour

Now sift the flour over the egg mixture and fold it in carefully. Bake in 2 ungreased 9-inch layer cake pans at 325° for 35 minutes.

Orange Filling

Beat until stiff

2 egg whites

Gradually beat into the whites

¼ cup sugar

Mix together and then fold into the stiff egg whites

¾ cup orange juice   ½ cup sugar
1 tablespoon grated orange rind

Spread each layer of the cake with this mixture. This mixture will be rather thin, the better to soak into the cake. Set the cake in the refrigerator for at least two hours; it may be left overnight. Before serving, spread the bottom layer with whipped cream sweetened to taste with sugar and flavored with vanilla. Place the second layer on top, then cover it and the sides with the remaining whipped cream. 1 cup of heavy cream, whipped, should be sufficient to fill and frost the cake.

CAKE ROLLS

When is a cake not a cake? When it's a roll. These cake rolls are more festive in appearance than a cake, especially when presented on a jelly roll board, and lighter in texture than most cakes, being made with little or no flour, since they depend for their airy substance on eggs. And they consume less time to make than most cakes. There is no need for failure with cake rolls if a few simple rules are followed.

Grease a cookie sheet of required size, cover the sheet with waxed paper and then generously grease the waxed paper. Bake as directed for each cake, and immediately on removing from the oven, cover with a cold damp towel and place in the refrigerator to cool rapidly. This causes the cake to contract and makes it easy to peel off the waxed paper, and it keeps it moist so that it rolls easily after being filled. Roll lengthwise by picking up edges of towel and allowing the cake to fold over—the last roll should land it on the board. And when serving the roll, always cut on the diagonal—it is so much more attractive that way that it seems to taste twice as good.

NUT ROLL

9 eggs
1½ cups sugar
2¼ cups ground pecans
or walnuts
1½ teaspoons baking
powder

2 cups heavy cream, whipped
and flavored with vanilla
and sweetened with sugar
to taste
Confectioners' sugar

Separate the eggs. Beat the sugar into the yolks. Mix in the ground nuts and baking powder, and finally fold in the stiffly beaten egg whites. Grease a cookie sheet, 14 by 17. Cover with waxed paper and grease again. Spread the mixture evenly on the sheet. Bake for 15 to 20 minutes in a 375° oven, until golden brown on top. Remove from oven and immediately cover with a cloth that has been wrung out in ice-cold water. Put into the refrigerator until completely cooled. Loosen with a spatula from the cookie sheet. Now turn the whole upside down so that the towel is on the bottom. Lift off the cookie sheet and carefully pull off the waxed paper. Cut off the crisp edges with a sharp knife. Spread the whole surface with whipped cream that has been sweetened to taste with sugar and flavored with vanilla. Pick up one side of the towel and roll the cake slowly lengthwise onto a board or serving plate. Dust the top with confectioners' sugar and keep in the refrigerator until time to serve.

JELLY ROLL

6 eggs
1 cup sugar
1 teaspoon vanilla

1 cup sifted cake flour
1 teaspoon baking powder
¼ teaspoon salt
Jelly or jam to fill roll

Separate eggs. Beat the yolks until they are light, and then gradually add the sugar. Continue beating until the mixture is creamy. Add the vanilla, resift the flour with the baking powder, and then sift over the egg mixture and beat until the batter is smooth. Beat the egg whites and salt until stiff, fold them into the batter. Grease a cookie sheet or jelly roll pan, 10 by 15 inches, spread it with waxed paper and grease again. Bake at 375° for 15 minutes, or until a toothpick inserted in the cake comes out clean. Cover with a damp cold towel and put in the refrigerator until cooled. Loosen the pan with a spatula, turn the whole upside down so that the towel is on the bottom. Carefully peel off the waxed paper. Spread the cake with any desired jam or jelly—a red one is quite attractive. Take hold of one side of the towel and roll the cake lengthwise slowly onto a board or plate.

STRAWBERRY OR RASPBERRY ROLL

Make cake according to directions for Jelly Roll in preceding recipe. Spread the cake with sweetened whipped cream into which has been folded a cup of sweetened crushed berries. Roll the cake onto a board, cover the top with sweetened whipped cream and garnish with whole berries. 1½ cups of heavy cream should be sufficient for whipping.

CHOCOLATE ROLL NO. 1

8 *eggs*
1 *cup sugar*
1½ *tablespoons cake flour*
4 *tablespoons Dutch cocoa*
1 *teaspoon baking powder*

2 *cups heavy cream, whipped and flavored with vanilla and sweetened with sugar to taste*
Confectioners' sugar

1 *bar sweet chocolate*

Separate the eggs. Beat the egg yolks until they are light. Beat in the sugar gradually and continue beating until creamy. Sift and then measure the flour and the cocoa. Add the baking powder and resift into the egg mixture. Stir until smooth. Beat the egg whites until stiff and fold them into the batter. Spread the batter evenly on a 14- by 17-inch cookie sheet that has been greased, covered with waxed paper, and greased again. Bake at 375° for 15 minutes, or until a toothpick comes out clean. Remove from oven and cover with a towel that has been wrung out in ice water. Cool in the refrigerator. Loosen from the cookie sheet with a spatula and then turn the roll upside down on the towel. Lift off the cookie sheet, and carefully peel off the waxed paper. Spread the entire surface with whipped cream that has been sweetened to taste with sugar and flavored with vanilla. Take hold of one side of the towel, and, lifting gently, roll the cake onto a board. Dust the top of the roll with confectioners' sugar and garnish with curls of sweet chocolate. To make the chocolate curls, run a vegetable scraper over the surface of a bar of sweet chocolate.

CHOCOLATE ROLL NO. 2

This roll is richer and moister than the preceding one and more unusual in taste and texture.

6 *large eggs*	1½ *cups heavy cream,*
1 *cup sugar*	*whipped until stiff,*
7 *ounces semi-sweet baking*	*sweetened to taste with*
chocolate	*sugar and flavored with*
3 *tablespoons cold water*	*vanilla*

Separate the eggs. Beat the yolks until frothy and then gradually beat in the sugar. Continue to beat until the consistency is light and creamy. Break up chocolate into pieces, place in saucepan, and add the water. Stir over a low heat until the chocolate dissolves. Do not permit it to cook. Stir chocolate into the egg mixture. Beat the egg whites until stiff and shiny and fold them into the mixture. Grease a 10- by 15-inch cookie sheet; cover with waxed paper and grease again. Spread the mixture evenly on top. Bake for 10 minutes at 375° and then 5 minutes at 300°. Remove from oven and cover top with a towel which has been wrung out in cold water. Cool. Remove towel and loosen roll from the tin. Turn out onto the cloth and carefully peel off the waxed paper. Spread with the whipped cream and roll, using the towel to roll it onto itself. Dust the top with confectioners' sugar. Serve on a long wooden board.

DOBOS TORTA
(MANY-LAYERED CAKE)

This is a famous confection that originated in Hungary. It is very rich and very impressive and not too difficult to make, if you have the patience to go through the various steps involved. It should be made at least a day before it is to be served, even better if allowed to stand two or three days. If you want the torta to be round, you will need an 8- to 9-inch layer pan. It is just as handsome if in a loaf shape, and it is much more convenient to make, for you can bake the cake on two baking sheets, cut it into 4- or 5-inch-wide strips, and stack the strips. You will want at least 8 layers.

5 eggs, separated	⅛ teaspoon salt
½ cup sugar	½ cup sifted cake flour

Beat the egg whites until stiff. Using the unwashed beaters, beat together the egg yolks, sugar, and salt until the mixture is thick and lemon-colored. Fold this into the beaten whites. Sift the flour over this mixture and gradually fold it in. Spread the batter ¼ inch thick in 8-inch layer pans or on 2 baking sheets that have been greased, spread with waxed paper, and greased again. Bake at 400° for 10 minutes. When done the cake should be a light gold color. Turn out of the pans and carefully pull off the paper.

Chocolate Cream Filling

6 *egg yolks*
1 *cup sugar*
¼ *pound semi-sweet choco-*
late, melted over hot water
¾ *cup butter*

Beat the egg yolks and sugar in top of a double boiler and cook over hot water, stirring constantly until mixture is thick. Remove from heat and stir in the melted chocolate. Beat until cool, then beat the butter in very thoroughly.

Put the layers together with this filling, saving enough to cover the sides of the cake. Leave off the top layer until it has been glazed.

Glaze

¾ *cup sugar*   1 *tablespoon butter*

Melt the butter and sugar in a small heavy pan, stir until golden, and then pour and spread it over the single top layer which has been set apart. Let cool for just a minute and then, with a sharp knife dipped in hot water, mark through the glaze the number of pieces into which you wish to cut the cake. (Once the glaze is hardened it is impossible to cut through it without crushing the cake.) Place the glazed layer carefully on the other filled layers and spread the reserved filling on the sides. Store in the refrigerator until time to serve.

CHOCOLATE ALMOND TORTE

Here is another Hungarian and Austrian dessert. It is just as rich as the Dobos Torta, and although not quite as impressive looking, it is, I think, even better tasting.

8 *eggs separated*
1 *cup sugar*
¼ *pound semi-sweet choco-late, melted over hot water*
½ *cup fine dry bread crumbs*
1 *cup blanched, crushed almonds*
1 *cup apricot jam*

Beat the egg whites until stiff. With the unwashed beaters (this is to save work), beat together the egg yolks and sugar until thick and lemon-colored. Stir the melted chocolate, crumbs, and crushed almonds into the egg yolk mixture and then fold in the stiff whites. Spread in three 8-inch layer pans or on one 10-by-15 baking sheet, greasing the pans first, lining them with waxed paper, and greasing again. Bake in a slow oven, 325°, for 30 minutes, or until the cake springs back when pressed lightly. Turn out of the pans and remove the paper at once. Put the layers together with apricot jam. If cake has been baked on a sheet, cut it into 3 strips and put these together with the jam. Cover sides and top with Coffee Cream Frosting.

Coffee Cream Frosting

6 *egg yolks*
⅓ *cup very strong coffee*
¾ *cup sugar*
¾ *cup sweet butter*

Beat together in top of a double boiler the eggs, coffee, and sugar. Cook, stirring constantly until mixture thickens. Cool to room temperature. Add butter bit by bit, and beat until thick enough to spread.

CHESTNUT TORTE

If you like chestnuts you will like this; if not, you won't. And if you do like them, the first crisp days of fall are when you will most likely get hungry for them, and on such a day, this would be a perfect dessert.

¾ cup chestnut purée
1 cup flour, sifted
1 teaspoon baking powder

6 tablespoons butter
⅔ cup sugar
1 teaspoon vanilla

6 eggs, separated

Prepare the chestnut purée by boiling 1 pound of chestnuts for 20 to 30 minutes, or until tender. Drain and peel. Put the meat through a fine meat chopper or purée them in an electric blender.

Resift the flour with the baking powder three times. Cream the butter and sugar until light, add the chestnut purée and vanilla, and beat well. Add the egg yolks, one at a time, and beat well after each addition. In a separate bowl, beat the egg whites until stiff. Fold the stiff whites into the chestnut mixture. Sift the dry ingredients on top of the mixture and carefully fold in. Bake in a greased 9-by-12 pan at 350° for 45 minutes. Lining the pan with greased wax paper will facilitate removing torte from pan. Cool in the pan for 10 minutes and then turn out onto a cake rack. Cool. Serve with whipped cream sweetened to taste and flavored with vanilla.

GREEK ALMOND TORTE

A most delicious way to use up accumulated egg whites. Egg whites can be kept in a closed glass jar in the refrigerator for as long as a month, and since so many recipes, especially for sauces, call for egg yolks, it is a good idea to have on hand a jar for saving the whites to be used for angel food cakes, meringues, and for this very special and easy-to-make torte.

1¼ *cups egg whites (about*   *and finely grated or*
    10 *whites)*   *ground*
½ *cup sugar*   2 *tablespoons flour*
½ *pound almonds, blanched*

Beat the whites until they stand in soft peaks, then gradually beat in the sugar and continue to beat until the whites stand in firm peaks. Carefully fold in the finely grated almonds and the flour. Grease three 10-inch cake pans or one large flat cookie sheet, line with wax paper and grease again. Spread the batter evenly in the pans and bake in a slow oven, 250°, for 1½ hours. Remove the cakes from the pans and cool. Gently peel off the waxed paper. If the torte has been baked on a cookie sheet, cut into thirds crosswise and put the three layers together with a cream filling or with sweetened and flavored whipped cream. Cover the top with sweetened and flavored whipped cream and decorate with shaved sweet or semi-sweet chocolate. A Crème Anglaise makes a very delicious filling (recipe below), but a Standard Cream Filling (see recipe) is also good.

CRÈME ANGLAISE

1 *tablespoon gelatin*   ½ *cup sugar*
¼ *cup cold water*   1 *cup scalded milk*
4 *egg yolks*   2 *egg whites beaten stiff*
⅛ *teaspoon salt*   1 *cup heavy cream whipped*
        1 *teaspoon vanilla or rum*

Soften the gelatin in the cold water. Beat the yolks, salt, and sugar together until creamy, gradually stir in the hot milk, return to a low flame and stir until mixture coats the spoon. Remove from fire. Add the softened gelatin and stir until dissolved. Cool until mixture is just beginning to set, fold in the stiffly beaten whites and the whipped cream. Flavor with vanilla or rum. When set, spread between layers of torte. Store in the refrigerator until serving time. The torte may be made and filled a day in advance. Spread the top with whipped cream, and decorate with chocolate only a few hours before serving.

CHOCOLATE FUDGE CAKE

An old-fashioned fudge cake that is as rich, moist, and flavorful today as it was way back before anyone dreamed of cake mixes.

½ cup butter
1¼ cups brown sugar, not too firmly packed
2 eggs
3 ounces unsweetened chocolate, melted
2 cups sifted cake flour
2½ teaspoons baking powder
½ teaspoon salt
1¼ cups milk
1 teaspoon vanilla

Cream the butter and brown sugar together. Add the eggs, one at a time, beating thoroughly after each addition. Beat in the melted chocolate gradually. Sift the cake flour, baking powder, and salt together, and then add alternately with the milk to the first mixture. Add vanilla. Beat just until smooth. Spread batter evenly in two 8-inch greased layer cake pans. Bake at 350° for 25 to 30 minutes, or until cake tests done. Cool in pans. Remove from pans and put layers together with Chocolate Peppermint Frosting, reserving enough of the frosting to cover sides and top.

Chocolate Peppermint Frosting

½ cup cocoa	1 teaspoon vanilla
2¾ cups sifted confectioners sugar	1 cup heavy cream
⅛ teaspoon salt	¼ cup crushed peppermint stick candy

Blend cocoa, sugar, salt, and vanilla with the heavy cream. Beat until thick enough to spread. Stir in the crushed peppermint stick candy.

ALMOND MERINGUE WITH CHOCOLATE FILLING

This is a classic French dessert called *Gâteau Rolla*. It is a pretty way to end a meal and a very sweet one—too sweet perhaps for some, but quite satisfying for others. The directions may sound complicated but are in practice quite simple and foolproof.

5 egg whites	¾ cup ground or grated almonds (use a nut grinder or grater, not a meat grinder, for the nuts will become oily)
⅛ teaspoon salt	
1 cup sugar	
1 teaspoon vanilla	

Beat the whites with the salt until they are stiff and are standing in peaks. Beat in gradually, one tablespoon at a time, ¾ cup of sugar, and continue to beat until the meringue is thick and very smooth. Fold in gently the remaining ¼ cup sugar, vanilla, and the ground or grated almonds.

Line two large flat baking sheets with waxed paper and

on each trace two 8-inch circles by putting an 8-inch plate on the sheets and tracing around it. Now spread each circle about ⅓ inch thick with the meringue and bake at 350° for 10 minutes. Remove the meringue circles from the paper to a counter or board to cool. Put the circles together with Chocolate Filling, reserving enough of the filling to frost the top and sides. Chill the cake in the refrigerator for at least 5 hours, preferably overnight. If you wish to gild the lily you can decorate the top just before serving by making a lattice work of inch strips of paper and sprinkle with confectioners' sugar. Remove the paper strips and the sugar will have formed a design on the cake.

Chocolate Filling

2 egg whites
⅔ cup sugar
¼ cup cocoa

¼ cup melted baking chocolate
1 cup sweet butter

Combine the egg whites and sugar in the top of a double boiler and beat over boiling water until smooth and thick, or about 3 or 4 minutes. Stir in the cocoa and the chocolate which has been melted over hot water. Beat in the cup of butter bit by bit. Chill the cream for at least an hour before spreading on the meringues.

ALMOND MERINGUE WITH FRESH BERRIES OR FRUIT

This dessert is just as decorative as the preceding meringue but is less sweet. Fresh fruit and meringues take naturally to each other.

Make the meringue according to directions for Almond Meringue with Chocolate Filling (see recipe).

Whip 2 cups heavy cream until stiff, sweeten to taste with sugar, and flavor with vanilla. Divide the whipped cream in half. Into one portion fold 2 cups of sliced fresh peaches, strawberries, or raspberries, or a combination of these or other fresh fruits. When ready to serve, put the four circles of meringue together with the fruit and cream mixture. Spread the sides and top of cake with the other portion of whipped cream and garnish with whole berries or slices of fruit.

CHERRY-TOPPED CHEESECAKE

Cheesecake recipes are infinite in their variety. Most cheesecake recipes call for a pastry crust or a heavy crumb crust. I think a heavy crust detracts from the cake and much prefer just to line the pan with fine dry zwieback or graham cracker crumbs. Butter the pan generously, pour in the dry crumbs, and roll the pan around until the sides and bottom are coated.

1¼ pounds cream cheese
(you may use ½ cream
cheese and ½ finely
mashed cottage cheese;
this gives a less rich cake)
⅞ cup sugar
1½ tablespoons flour
1 teaspoon each grated

orange and lemon rind
¼ teaspoon vanilla
3 whole eggs
2 tablespoons heavy cream or
sour cream
Canned sweet black (or semi-
sweet red) cherries
2 teaspoons cornstarch

Have the cheese at room temperature. Combine the cheese, sugar, flour, rind, and vanilla, and beat until thoroughly blended. Add the whole eggs one at a time, beating after each addition; fold in the cream. Pour into a crumb-lined, or if you prefer, a pastry-lined, 8-inch spring mold. Bake in a hot (450°) oven for 10 minutes. Reduce heat to 200° and continue baking for 45 minutes.

Cool the cake and cover the top closely with canned sweet black cherries or with the canned semi-sweet red cherries. Put 1½ cups of the juice into a pan, and when boiling, slowly stir in 2 teaspoons of cornstarch that has been dissolved in a little of the cold juice. Stir until mixture thickens. Remove from fire and cool to room temperature. Glaze the cherries completely with this sauce. Chill the cake before serving.

FRESH STRAWBERRY CHEESECAKE

Make cheesecake as directed for Cherry-Topped Cheesecake above. Cover top of cake closely with whole fresh strawberries. Mash ½ cup strawberries and combine them with 1 cup sugar and ¾ cup water. Bring the mixture to a boil. Dissolve 2 teaspoons cornstarch in 2 tablespoons cold water and stir it into the strawberry juice. Boil, stirring until thick. Cool and spread it evenly over the strawberry topping. Chill the cake before serving.

APPLE CAKE

4 medium-sized apples	¾ cup sugar
½ cup sugar	1½ teaspoons baking powder
1 tablespoon flour	¼ cup butter or margarine
2 tablespoons cinnamon	2 eggs, well beaten
1 cup sifted cake flour	⅓ cup milk
½ teaspoon vanilla	

Peel and core the apples and cut into even slices. Steam the apples in a colander over hot water until they just begin to get a transparent look. Roll the slices in a mixture of the sugar, flour, and cinnamon. If using a fast cooking apple, omit the steaming. Into a mixing bowl resift the flour, sugar, baking powder. Cut in the butter or margarine and mix well with a pastry cutter until the consistency of a very coarse meal. Gradually add the beaten eggs mixed with the milk and vanilla. Blend together thoroughly. Pour the batter into a greased and lightly floured 8-inch square cake pan. Now arrange the sugar- and cinnamon-coated apple slices in neat overlapping rows on top. Bake at 375° for 40 minutes or until cake tests done. Serve cold, topped with sweetened and flavored whipped cream.

Custards and Puddings

CUSTARDS AND PUDDINGS are an important and interesting category of desserts. They depend primarily on milk, eggs, and cream, items which are essential to our daily diet and items which, when fresh and handled correctly, make delightful eating. There are a few simple rules to remember when working with milk or with cream and eggs. First, for any given dessert, do not tamper with the proportion of milk, cream, and eggs called for, either in an attempt to economize or to be more lavish. Too many eggs in proportion to the liquid is likely to give you a curdled mass; too few eggs will give a runny custard. True custards are thickened by eggs alone, and a perfect custard is smooth, creamy, and delicate, the thickness depending on the type. Puddings have an additional thickening agent, flour or cornstarch, and are not so touchy to prepare, but care must be taken when adding the eggs to the hot mixture. Always add a bit of the hot mixture to the eggs to warm them before stirring them into the pan of hot mixture. If you do not, the eggs will cook immediately on being poured into the pudding, leaving you with a thickened milk base full of scrambled eggs.

Second, remember that eggs coagulate at a very very

low temperature. Cooking at too high a heat or for too long a time is the most common cause of failure in making a custard. When making a boiled custard, stir over low heat until mixture just coats the spoon. Do not permit it to boil or it will curdle past the point of being edible. Since most foods have to boil and bubble to cook, this is a characteristic of eggs that it is well not to forget. This is also true when thickening a sauce with egg yolks. Never boil the sauce after stirring in the yolks. In the case of a baked custard, the bowl or cups of custard must be placed in a pan of water and baked at a low temperature. If there is danger of the water in the pan boiling, add a bit of ice or ice water to it to keep the temperature down. A baked custard that is porous or which separates into curd and liquid has been baked at too high a heat or for too long.

Third, the manner in which the eggs and milk or cream have been mixed and beaten affects the consistency of the custard. If the eggs are well beaten instead of just lightly beaten you will have a less firm custard, one which will be impossible to unmold. A foam forms on top with beating and this bakes into a beautiful brown topping. This is desirable for custard pies and for custard to be served in the baking cups. For a custard that you wish to unmold, such as a vanilla custard to serve with fruit or a caramel custard, the eggs must be only lightly mixed, for you do not want to incorporate air into them, since the less air beaten into the eggs, the firmer and smoother the custard.

These recipes yield enough for six servings.

CRÈME CARAMEL

A French classic, well deserving of its popularity, Crème Caramel is a custard so smooth and firm that it can be cut like a cake, and it's quite tempting in appearance with its brown caramel topping and sauce.

First, coat a 1-quart soufflé dish or glass casserole with caramel syrup:

1 *cup sugar*	⅓ *cup water*
	¼ *teaspoon cream of tartar*

Combine these ingredients in a heavy skillet or saucepan, and cook over low heat without stirring until the syrup turns amber, or a good lively brown. Now with the baking dish in one hand and the pan of syrup in the other, pour the syrup into the dish while you rotate it so that the sides and bottom are completely coated with the caramel. Set aside for the caramel to harden before pouring in the custard.

4 *whole eggs*	3 *cups hot milk*
6 *egg yolks*	1 *inch of vanilla bean or 1*
8 *tablespoons sugar*	*teaspoon of vanilla*
¼ *teaspoon salt*	

Break the eggs into a bowl, add the sugar and salt, and toss lightly with a fork until just barely mixed. Slowly stir in the hot milk and vanilla. If using a vanilla bean, put it into the milk while heating it, discard before adding to the eggs. Pour into the soufflé dish with the hardened caramel lining, place in a pan of water, and bake at 275° for 2 hours or until firm. When custard is done, a small pointed knife should come out clean; or press gently with a finger tip, and if no liquid breaks through it is done. Cool and then chill in the refrigerator. Unmold on a platter to serve. To unmold, run a sharp knife all around the edge. Place the serving dish on top and, holding tightly, tip the whole upside down. Lift off the baking dish, and you will have a lovely gold and brown mold.

BAKED VANILLA CUSTARD

Make a custard as directed in preceding recipe and pour it into a buttered soufflé dish or glass casserole instead of a caramelized one. Bake, chill, and unmold as directed. Garnish with sliced fruit or berries.

BAKED CHOCOLATE CUSTARD

Follow directions for the custard in Crème Caramel (see recipe). When heating the milk, add 6 ounces semisweet chocolate and stir until dissolved. Pour into a buttered baking dish and bake, chill, and unmold as directed.

POTS DE CRÈME, VANILLA OR CHOCOLATE

These little French pots of cream are smooth and delicious and so easy to make as a dessert. Given below is the recipe for the Chocolate Pots de Crème. To make the Vanilla Pots de Crème merely omit the chocolate and add ½ cup sugar and one teaspoon vanilla. If using vanilla bean, put it into the milk while scalding it and let it stand for 5 minutes to absorb the full flavor.

1 *cup milk*　　　　　　　　½ *pound sweet baking choc-*
1 *cup cream*　　　　　　　　　*olate, grated*
　　　　　　　　6 *egg yolks*

Scald the milk and cream, add the grated chocolate, and cook the mixture, stirring, until the chocolate is melted. Beat the egg yolks until light, and after stirring a bit of the hot mixture into them, slowly stir them into the milk mixture, stirring constantly. Continue to cook over a low heat for just a few minutes, or until mixture just barely coats the spoon. Strain the mixture into *pots de crème,* little cups made specially for this dessert, or small custard cups. Set them in a pan of water and bake in a 300° oven for 15 to 25 minutes or until a pointed knife inserted in the center comes out clean. Cool and chill. Serve each little pot topped with whipped cream.

CRÈME BRÛLÉE

This is the richest of all the custards, a very smooth cream topped with crispy caramelized sugar. The custard must be thick and firm enough to spoon out but not of a "set" consistency.

3 *cups thick cream*　　　　6 *egg yolks*
1 *inch of vanilla bean or* 1　1½ *cups sugar*
　teaspoon vanilla extract

Heat the cream with the vanilla bean in a heavy pan to just past lukewarm. If using vanilla extract, add it to the mixture at the end. Beat the eggs with ½ cup of the sugar until very creamy and light. Mix in the warm cream very slowly and carefully. Return to the thick pan, stir over a low heat until the mixture coats the back of a spoon. Pour into a shallow (2-inch) glass dish. Place in the refrigerator to set for at least 8 hours, or overnight. When ready to serve, cover top completely with the remaining cup of sugar so that none of the cream shows through. Place the dish on a bed of crushed ice and place under a broiler until all the sugar is caramelized.

STANDARD CREAM PUDDING OR FILLING

This is an excellent cream for use in all cream pies, such as coconut cream, banana cream, or cream with a fruit or berry topping. It is also ideal for such desserts as trifles or filled cake.

3 *egg yolks*	2½ *tablespoons cornstarch*
⅓ *cup sugar*	1 *tablespoon butter*
⅓ *teaspoon salt*	2 *cups scalded milk*

1 *teaspoon vanilla*

Beat the yolks until light, then beat in the sugar, salt, cornstarch, and butter. Add a bit of the hot milk to these ingredients and then carefully stir them back into the pan of milk. Cook over low heat, stirring constantly until it thickens, that is, until a spoon pulled through will leave a slight path. Add the vanilla. Cool and it is ready to use.

When making a coconut or banana cream pie, add the coconut or bananas as soon as you remove from fire.

BAKED CUSTARD FOR SAUCES

Why this should sometimes be referred to as a boiled custard is a bit of a mystery, for at no time must it be allowed to boil.

4 *egg yolks*	⅛ *teaspoon salt*
¼ *cup sugar*	2 *cups scalded milk*

1 *teaspoon vanilla or other desired flavoring*

Beat the egg yolks slightly, add the sugar and salt. Stir a little of the hot milk into the yolks to warm them and then carefully stir the egg mixture into the pan of milk.

Cook, stirring constantly over very low heat until the custard coats the back of a spoon. Never on any account allow it to boil or it will curdle badly. In fact, if allowed to stay on the heat for even a second after it coats the spoon it will curdle a little and not be as good or as attractive to serve. Add flavoring. Strain and cool the custard before using. It will thicken appreciably as it cools.

FLOATING ISLAND

A frothy light meringue floating on a pool of creamy custard sauce. This is frequently thought of as invalid fare. Although it is undoubtedly excellent as such, it tastes and looks just as good to noninvalids.

>   6 *egg whites*
>   ¾ *cup sugar*
>   1 *teaspoon vanilla*

Beat the egg whites until they stand in soft peaks, then add the sugar, a tablespoon at a time, and continue beating until stiff and glossy. Add the vanilla and, if you want variety, you may fold in ½ cup fine ground nuts, preferably almonds. Turn the mixture into a greased and sugared quart mold. Place the mold in a pan of hot water and bake in a slow oven (275°) for 20 to 30 minutes or until firm. Cool the meringue, unmold it in a glass bowl, and gently pour around it a chilled custard sauce made as directed in the preceding recipe. The meringue will rise and float on the custard.

CARAMEL FLOATING ISLAND

An interesting and delicious variation on Floating Island. Make the meringue as directed for Floating Island in

preceding recipe. Make a caramel syrup as for Crème
Caramel (see recipe). Coat a quart mold with the caramel
syrup. When the caramel is set, fill with the meringue and
bake in a slow oven (275°) for 20 to 30 minutes, or until
set. Cool and unmold on a glass bowl and gently pour
on custard sauce until the meringue rises and floats.

HOT ZABAGLIONE SAUCE

Zabaglione Sauce is of Italian origin, but it is internation-
ally known as a superb accompaniment for fresh, frozen, or
stewed fruit and for various puddings and cakes. Some
like it hot, some like it cold, and some like it both ways, so
I am giving recipes for both versions.

6 egg yolks
⅞ cup sugar
½ teaspoon vanilla
½ cup sherry

Beat the egg yolks with 1 tablespoon of the sugar until
they are thick and pale lemon-colored. Add the vanilla
and then gradually beat in the sherry alternately with the
remaining sugar. Place over warm water and cook over
low heat, beating steadily until thick and hot. Serve immediately.

COLD ZABAGLIONE SAUCE

6 egg yolks
⅛ teaspoon salt
¾ cup sugar
Juice of ½ lemon
¾ cup sherry
2 teaspoons brandy
1 cup heavy cream, whipped

Beat the egg yolk, salt, sugar, and lemon juice together
until light and fluffy. Place in top of double boiler and
cook, stirring constantly until thick. Remove from heat

and gradually stir in the sherry and brandy. Cool the mixture and then fold in the whipped cream. Keep in the refrigerator until ready to serve.

PASTRY CREAM I

This is the most useful and versatile of creams. It is not a dessert in itself but is an important part of innumerable desserts. Fresh fruit tarts are better if there is a layer of pastry cream between the pastry and the fruit. It makes an excellent filling for cream puffs, éclairs, and napoleons, or for cakes, babas, and tortes, and is superb in combination with poached peaches and pears.

1 *egg*
1 *egg yolk*
2 *tablespoons flour*
3 *tablespoons sugar*
1 *tablespoon gelatin*
3 *tablespoons cold water*
1 *cup hot milk*

2 *stiffly beaten egg whites*
4 *tablespoons whipped cream (optional, gives added richness)*
vanilla or rum to flavor to taste

Beat together the egg, egg yolk, flour, and sugar. Dissolve the gelatin in 3 tablespoons cold water and stir in. Carefully and slowly stir in the hot milk. Cook, stirring over a low fire until the mixture comes to a boil and is thickened and smooth. Cool and when just beginning to set, fold in the stiffly beaten egg whites and the optional whipped cream. Flavor with vanilla or rum.

PASTRY CREAM II

This version of pastry cream is made without gelatin and so it has a less firm consistency.

½ cup sugar   ¼ cup flour
4 egg yolks   1½ cups hot milk
Vanilla to flavor

Beat together the sugar and egg yolks until they are creamy. Stir in the flour. Gradually stir in the hot milk. Cook over a low fire, stirring vigorously until it reaches the boiling point, but do not permit it to boil. Flavor with vanilla extract. If you prefer to use vanilla bean, put the bean into the milk before heating and remove the bean from the custard before cooling it.

CHOCOLATE MOUSSE

Just the dish for chocolate lovers.

7 eggs, separated   ⅓ cup sugar
¾ pound bittersweet   7 tablespoons cold water
  chocolate   4 tablespoons cognac

Beat the egg yolks until thick and lemon colored. Combine the chocolate, sugar and water in a heavy saucepan and stir over a low fire until the chocolate is completely melted. Add a bit of the hot chocolate to the yolks and then gradually stir the yolks into the melted chocolate. Add the cognac and cook, stirring, until mixture is thickened. Cool to room temperature. Beat the egg whites until stiff and fold them into the chocolate mixture. Spoon the mousse into small cups and chill for at least 5 hours. Serve in the cups, topped with sweetened whipped cream.

CHOCOLATE MOUSSE WITH MACAROONS

Make a chocolate mousse as directed in preceding recipe but omit the cognac from the mousse. Take ¾ pound of almond macaroons and soak them in ½ cup of cognac. Rinse out a mold with water, spoon in a layer of mousse, cover with a layer of cognac-soaked macaroon, again a layer of mousse, and then a layer of the macaroon. Chill for at least 5 hours. Unmold on a serving platter, cover top and sides with whipped cream that has been sweetened to taste and flavored with vanilla. Garnish if desired with curls of sweet chocolate. To make chocolate, run a carrot scraper over a bar of sweet chocolate. Almond macaroons can usually be obtained at a bakery shop.

MOCHA RUM CHARLOTTE

A chocolate charlotte with a difference, the difference being the coffee and rum, but only the cook will know this. The diners will marvel and wonder how to describe the wonderful concoction they are eating.

½ cup water
½ cup sugar
5 tablespoons rum
30 ladyfingers to line sides and bottoms of 6 individual molds and to cover tops
5 ounces semi-sweet chocolate
1 cup strong coffee
¼ cup butter
5 egg yolks, slightly beaten
5 egg whites, stiffly beaten
¾ cup whipped cream, sweetened to taste, and flavored with vanilla

Combine the water, sugar, and ½ of the rum and boil together for 4 minutes, cool, and add the remaining rum. Line the bottom and sides of 6 small molds with ladyfingers that have been soaked in the rum syrup. If you do not have individual molds you may use cups for this purpose. And strips of sponge cake or angel food may be substituted for the ladyfingers.

Melt the semi-sweet chocolate in the coffee and cook it for 5 minutes. Remove from the heat. Add the butter and gradually stir in the egg yolks, after first warming them with a bit of the hot mixture. Mix well. Fold in the stiffly beaten whites. Pour this coffee-chocolate mixture into the molds and cover with more of the rum soaked ladyfingers. Chill for at least 12 hours. Unmold the charlottes, sprinkle them with the remaining syrup, cover with whipped cream and garnish with curls of sweet chocolate. Make the chocolate curls by running a vegetable scraper over a bar of sweet chocolate.

Bavarian Creams and Other Molded Gelatin Desserts

THESE DELICATE, airy creams, molded in beautiful shapes and garnished with a flair, are truly the most elegant of desserts. They serve as a delightful and delicious ending to a meal at any season but really come into their own in summer when even the most heat-jaded appetite is won by their refreshing appearance and taste, and when you have an infinite variety of fresh fruits and berries to use as garnish or as the base of the cream.

These molded gelatin desserts are very simple to make and need no special skill or technique, but a few rules must be adhered to. The proportion of gelatin to liquid must not be tampered with. Gelatin must always first be softened in cold water and then completely dissolved, either by stirring it into a hot liquid or by stirring it over hot water. The cream must be cooled and allowed to reach the point of just beginning to set before the whipped cream or stiffly beaten egg whites, or both, are folded into it. The mold must be of proper size if the dessert is to be attractive. Rinse the mold with cold water before filling or butter lightly. The cream must be given ample time to set in the refrigerator before unmolding, at least four hours, but not too long a time, for this dessert does not age well. It is never as good or as pretty the second day.

Unmolding a gelatin dessert need not be tricky. When the cream is firm and well set, run a knife around the edge, dip the mold quickly into hot water, place the serving plate on top, and, grasping firmly, turn the whole over, gently lift off the mold and return the cream to the refrigerator until ready to garnish and serve. The color and flavor of Bavarian creams and gelatin fruit molds can be varied ad infinitum. For a starter, vanilla, chocolate, coffee, almond, ginger, rum, kirsch, Cointreau, peach, strawberry, raspberry, apricot, nectarine, and so on.

Charlotte Russe, an equally well-known name in the dessert world, is nothing more than a Bavarian cream extended with ladyfingers or fingers of sponge cake or angel food cake. Line a buttered mold with ladyfingers or strips of cake, cover the bottom of the mold with the same arranged in an attractive pattern, and fill the mold with a Bavarian cream.

These recipes yield six servings.

VANILLA BAVARIAN CREAM

This is perhaps the most useful of the creams, for it adapts itself to the largest variety of garnishes. Any fresh, frozen, or canned fruit or berry goes beautifully with it.

1 *envelope or tablespoon of gelatin*
2 *tablespoons cold water*
4 *egg yolks*
½ *cup sugar*
1 *cup milk, scalded*

1 *inch vanilla bean or 1 teaspoon vanilla extract*
1 *cup heavy cream, whipped*
Optional: 2 egg whites, stiffly beaten (this makes a lighter and less rich cream)

Soften the gelatin in the cold water. Beat the egg yolks with the sugar until light and pale lemon-colored. Pour the hot milk gradually over the egg mixture. Cook, stirring constantly, over a very low flame, or in the top of a double boiler over boiling water until it thickens and is very smooth. If using vanilla bean, put it into the milk while scalding and remove from custard before stirring in the gelatin. If using vanilla extract, stir in when removing from fire. Stir in the softened gelatin and stir until completely dissolved. Cool the cream. If in a hurry, cool over cracked ice; otherwise cool in the refrigerator. When the cream is just on the point of setting, fold in the whipped cream. If you wish a lighter cream, also fold in 2 stiffly beaten egg whites. Mold in any desired form. Chill for at least 4 hours. Loosen the edges with a knife, dip the bottom quickly in hot water, and unmold onto a serving platter. Garnish as desired.

COFFEE BAVARIAN CREAM AND CHOCOLATE BAVARIAN CREAM

Follow recipe for Vanilla Bavarian Cream but omit the vanilla and stir in with the gelatin 2 tablespoons coffee powder or extract. For chocolate flavor, stir in with the gelatin 2 ounces melted chocolate.

KIRSCH OR COINTREAU BAVARIAN CREAM

Follow recipe for Vanilla Bavarian Cream but omit the vanilla and flavor the whipped cream with 2 tablespoons of kirsch or 3 teaspoons of Cointreau.

ALMOND BAVARIAN CREAM

This is the most subtle of the Bavarian creams and, I think, the most delicious. It reaches its peak when served with fresh strawberries.

1 *tablespoon or envelope of gelatin*
¼ *cup cold water*
½ *cup almond paste (available in most food stores in cans; be certain to get the paste, not almond filling)*
1½ *cups milk*

4 *egg yolks*
1 *teaspoon vanilla*
1½ *cups heavy cream, whipped*
Optional: 2 egg whites stiffly beaten (this will make an airier cream and also increase the quantity)

Soften the gelatin in the cold water. In a saucepan combine the almond paste and the milk. Cook, stirring, over low heat until the paste has dissolved and the mixture is smooth. Beat the egg yolks, and after warming them with a little of the hot milk, stir them gradually into the saucepan with the milk and cook over very low heat until the custard is slightly thickened. Do not allow it to boil or even simmer. It should just coat spoon. Taste the custard for sweetness. The almond paste should have provided enough sweetening but if not, stir in sugar to taste. Stir in the softened gelatin and stir until completely dissolved. Stir the cream over cracked ice until it cools and just begins to set. Stir in the vanilla and the whipped cream and, if desired, the egg whites. Rinse a mold with cold water, shake off the excess drops of water, fill with the cream, and put into the refrigerator to chill and set, for at least 4 hours. Unmold onto a serving plate and garnish with strawberries and whipped cream or other fruit of your choice.

STRAWBERRY OR RASPBERRY BAVARIAN CREAM OR CHARLOTTE

The cream can be molded by itself or made into a charlotte by lining the mold with ladyfingers or strips of sponge or angel food cake; the latter makes a larger and more substantial dessert and, I think, a more satisfying one.

1½ quarts strawberries or raspberries	2 envelopes or tablespoons of gelatin
1 tablespoon lemon juice or kirsch	¼ cup cold water
¾ cup sugar	1½ cups heavy cream, whipped

Optional: 2 egg whites, stiffly beaten (if making a charlotte)

Wash and hull the berries. Save ½ quart for garnish. Mash one quart of the berries to a fine purée. Strain part of the purée of raspberries if you want to reduce the amount of seeds. Add the lemon juice and sugar and stir until sugar is completely dissolved. Soften the gelatin in the cold water in a small pan or metal cup, and then place it over hot water and stir until the gelatin is completely dissolved. Stir the gelatin into the fruit mixture and chill in refrigerator or stir over cracked ice until it is just beginning to set. Fold in the whipped cream, and, if making a charlotte, the stiffly beaten egg whites. Pour into a mold and chill for at least 4 hours. Unmold onto a serving plate and garnish with the whole fresh berries. (If making a charlotte, spread the sides and top with whipped cream that has been sweetened to taste and flavored with vanilla before garnishing with the berries.)

PEACH CHARLOTTE

This dessert is always a success and always a mystery because of the subtle flavor and aroma imparted by the rum.

1½ envelopes or tablespoons of gelatin

⅓ cup cold water

1½ cups mashed fresh peaches or frozen peaches

½ to ¾ cup sugar (taste for amount of sugar needed; if using frozen peaches they will, of course, be already sweetened)

3 tablespoons rum

1 cup heavy cream, whipped

2 egg whites, stiffly beaten

Angel food cake to line the sides and bottom of mold

Soften the gelatin in the cold water and then dissolve it over hot water. Mix the dissolved gelatin with the mashed peaches, sugar, and rum. When using frozen peaches be sure they are at room temperature before stirring in the gelatin, for if it is stirred into icy peaches, it will immediately set and form a gummy ball in the middle of the peaches. When the cream is just on the point of setting, fold in the whipped cream and stiffly beaten egg whites. Line a mold with the strips of angel food cake; this will require about ½ of a 9-inch angel food. Pour the cream into the mold and chill for at least 4 hours. Unmold onto a serving platter, spread the top and sides with sweetened whipped cream and garnish with peach slices.

NESSELRODE CHARLOTTE

This is a lovely charlotte to serve in the wintertime when you want a molded dessert but fresh berries and fruit are not available.

1 tablespoon or envelope gelatin
¼ cup cold water
¾ cup scalded milk
⅓ cup sugar
⅛ teaspoon salt
½ teaspoon vanilla
2 tablespoons rum

1 cup heavy cream, whipped
1 cup bottled nesselrode mix
1 package ladyfingers or equivalent amount of sponge cake cut in finger-sized strips

Soften the gelatin in the cold water. Add the gelatin to the scalded milk and stir until completely dissolved. Stir in the sugar and salt. Add the vanilla and rum and set in a pan of cracked ice, and when it begins to set, whip it well with a rotary beater and then fold in the whipped cream and nesselrode mix. Line a quart mold with the ladyfingers or sponge cake, fill with the cream, and chill until firm—at least 5 hours. Unmold, serve garnished with whipped cream and curls of sweet chocolate.

PINK AND WHITE BAVARIAN CREAM

You can make this cream pink and white or any two colors you choose. You could make two Bavarian creams, for example, strawberry and vanilla. Allow them to set slightly, then divide your mold in half with a piece of greased cardboard. Pour one cream on each side, allow to stand in the refrigerator for five minutes and then gently pull out the cardboard. You can, of course, divide the mold into any number of sections and fill each section with a different-flavored cream. Chocolate and vanilla or coffee are good combinations, as are kirsch and peach.

APRICOT GELATIN

Refreshingly lovely in appearance and in taste. The apricot has a tantalizing flavor and should be more popular as a basis for desserts. Try this and I am sure you will be looking for other ways to end your meals with apricots.

1 2-pound 14-ounce can whole peeled apricots
2 oranges
1 lemon
½ cup sugar
¼ teaspoon almond extract
2 tablespoons or envelopes of gelatin

½ cup cold water
½ cup boiling water
½ cup almonds, blanched and split in half for garnish
1 cup heavy cream, whipped for garnish

Drain and reserve the juice from the apricots. Remove the pits and mash the apricots. Squeeze the juice from the oranges and the lemon and strain into the apricot juice. Stir in the sugar, apricot pulp, and almond extract. Soften the gelatin in the cold water, add it to the boiling water and stir until completely dissolved. Stir into the apricot mixture. Mix well and pour into 1½-quart mold. Chill until well set. When ready to serve, unmold onto a serving plate. Spread sides and top with sweetened whipped cream that has been flavored with vanilla or with apricot brandy, and decorate with the almonds. If you prefer, you can decorate with apricot halves instead of almonds.

COLD CARAMEL SOUFFLÉ

This is an impressive dessert and, for caramel lovers, a great treat. It should come to the table standing high above the dish, just like a baked soufflé.

¾ cup sugar
1 tablespoon corn syrup
½ cup cold water
4 eggs
3 egg yolks
1 tablespoon or envelope
  gelatin

¾ cup very strong hot coffee
1 cup heavy cream, whipped
¼ cup brandy
3 egg whites, stiffly beaten
Chopped nuts (optional)

Put half of the sugar into a heavy pan with the syrup and ¼ cup water. Stir until sugar is dissolved and then cook without stirring over a medium flame until the sugar makes a good dark caramel. Add 4 tablespoons water and cool a little. Put the eggs and egg yolks into a bowl with ¼ cup sugar, and beat with an electric beater or by hand until thick and rather stiff. Soften the gelatin in cold water and then dissolve in the hot coffee. Stir the gelatin and coffee mixture into the egg mixture. Add ¼ of the whipped cream which has been flavored with the brandy. Fold in the stiffly beaten egg whites. Oil a soufflé dish, tie a 2-inch-deep collar of waxed paper around the dish to give it additional height. Pour in the mixture so that it comes right up to the very top of the collar. Chill until well set. Carefully remove the waxed paper, decorate the top with the remaining whipped cream and some chopped nuts. Serve directly from the soufflé dish.

CRÈME GÉNOISE

This festive and exotic dessert will be a triumph at any season. Although it is a cold molded dessert and is garnished with berries, either fresh or frozen, the addition of the brandy-soaked macaroons takes it out of the "typically summer" category.

8 *macaroons*
1/3 *cup brandy*
1 1/4 *cups rich milk*
1/4 *cup sugar*
Rind of 1/2 *orange, cut into fine strips*

1 *tablespoon gelatin*
1/4 *cup cold milk*
4 *egg yolks, beaten*
2 *egg whites, stiffly beaten*
1/2 *cup heavy cream, whipped*

Crush the macaroons and soak them in the brandy. Put the 1 1/4 cups milk, sugar, and orange rind into a saucepan and simmer over a low flame for 8 minutes. Soak the gelatin in the 1/4 cup cold milk and then stir into the hot mixture. Add a few drops of the hot mixture to the beaten yolks to warm them and then carefully stir them into the hot mixture and cook, stirring, over a low flame until the mixture just begins to thicken. Strain this custard over the brandy-soaked macaroons. Cool until it is just beginning to set, and then fold in the stiffly beaten whites and the whipped cream. Turn the mixture into a melon mold that has been dipped in cold water, and chill until firm, or at least 5 hours. Unmold onto a serving platter and garnish with sweetened strawberries or raspberries that have been flavored with brandy. If you do not have a melon mold, a glass casserole or bowl will serve as a mold.

ENGLISH TRIFLE

The trifle is a much maligned dessert. True, it can be a horrible mixture of leftovers or a mixture of horrible leftovers, but it need not be horrible at all even if leftovers are involved. It can and should be a delightful and delicious dessert.

2 *teaspoons gelatin*

1 *recipe of Cream Pudding (see recipe) or 1 package vanilla pudding mix made by directions on package*

2 *packages ladyfingers or equivalent amount of*

sponge cake cut into thin strips

Raspberry jam to spread liberally on the cake (or any jam of choice)

½ *cup brandy*

1 *cup heavy cream, whipped, to cover top and sides*

Soften the gelatin in cold water and then dissolve it in the hot pudding. Cool the pudding before proceeding with the trifle. Spread each ladyfinger or strip of cake generously with jam. Raspberry jam is very good, but any one of your favorite jams will do. A red-colored jam is, of course, quite attractive. Cover the bottom of a mold or a deep cake pan (8 by 4 by 3) with ladyfingers, sprinkle with some of the brandy, cover with a layer of the pudding. Now put down another layer of jam, spread ladyfingers or cake, again sprinkle with brandy, and cover with pudding. Continue until all the ingredients are used up. Set in the refrigerator for at least 5 hours. It is even better when allowed to stand overnight. Run a knife around edges to loosen from pan or mold. Turn out onto a serving plate. Cover top and sides with whipped cream sweetened to taste and flavored with vanilla.

CHARLOTTE AUX POMMES (APPLES)

This dessert does not exactly fit the definitions of a charlotte, but it is a well-known French dish, and it might be presumptuous to change the name. Since it is a hearty dessert and one that should be served hot, it is best served in cold or cool weather.

6¼ pounds tart apples
4 tablespoons butter
1 cup water
1 cup sugar

4 tablespoons lemon juice
6 tablespoons apricot jam
1 loaf firm white bread, un-
  sliced and slightly stale

¼ pound butter

Peel, core, and slice the apples. Heat butter in a large heavy saucepan, add the apples, water, sugar, and lemon juice. Cover and cook over a low heat until apples are mushy. Uncover, turn up heat and cook, stirring, until sauce is very thick, so thick that when you run a spoon through the center it leaves a path. Stir in the apricot jam.

Slice the bread quite thin and cut each slice in half. Melt ¼ pound butter and dip one side of each slice of bread in the butter and line the bottom and sides of a well-buttered casserole or mold. Cut the slices to fit the bottom of the dish exactly and have the slices lining the side overlapping. This makes a very attractive pattern when unmolded.

Spoon the applesauce into the bread-lined mold, cover the sauce with bread slices cut to fit shape of top. Have these slices dipped in butter on both sides. Bake at 375° for 45 minutes. Remove from oven. Turn out mold onto a serving platter. Do this carefully. Loosen edges with a knife. Put the plate on top of mold, grip firmly and turn over. After about 10 minutes the charlotte should slide out without collapsing. Lift off the plate and there you are with a hot golden mold ready to serve with an accompanying bowl of apricot sauce. To make the sauce, boil together 1 cup of apricot jam and 1 cup of water for 2 or 3 minutes; strain into a bowl and add kirsch to taste. The sauce may be either hot or cold, a matter of preference.

Frozen Desserts

THE FAVORITE AMERICAN DESSERT is ice cream, and with good reason. It is delicious, nutritious, and seems right after most main courses. But since it is so common in American homes it no longer seems a festive or fancy way to end a meal. There are many other frozen desserts, however, which are as refreshing and delicious as ice cream and have the added virtue of being unusual and partyish. These recipes yield six servings.

FROZEN VANILLA SOUFFLÉ

This is called a soufflé only because of its appearance. It is frozen in a soufflé dish with a 2-inch collar so that when the collar is removed, it comes to the table towering above the dish just as a soufflé does. This dessert is undoubtedly better when made with a vanilla bean, but don't let the lack of a bean deter you from making it, for vanilla extract does very well. Stir in the extract with the whipped cream.

4 egg yolks
1 cup sugar
1/8 teaspoon salt
1 cup milk

3-inch piece of vanilla bean or 2 teaspoons vanilla extract
1 cup light cream

2 cups heavy cream, whipped

Beat the egg yolks in a heavy saucepan until light and lemon-colored; gradually beat in the sugar and salt, and ¼ cup of the milk. Split the vanilla bean and place it in a pan with the light cream and the remaining ¾ cup of milk and heat to the boiling point. Cool and remove the bean, scraping out the inside of the bean into the milk. Stir the milk into the egg mixture and cook over a low heat, stirring constantly, until mixture coats the back of a spoon. Cool to room temperature and then fold in the whipped cream. Tie a 3-inch-deep band of tin foil around the outside at the top of a quart soufflé dish; fill with the mixture, and freeze for at least 6 hours. It may be made a day in advance. Remove the foil rim and garnish the top with curls of sweet chocolate. Make the curls by running a carrot scraper over a bar of sweet chocolate. Bring to the table in the dish. It will give the illusion of a hot soufflé.

FROZEN CHOCOLATE SOUFFLÉ

Follow directions for Frozen Vanilla Soufflé but add 8 ounces, or more or less according to your taste, of semi-sweet chocolate to the milk when heating it. Stir until chocolate is completely dissolved.

FROZEN COFFEE SOUFFLÉ

Follow directions for making Frozen Vanilla Soufflé, omitting the vanilla and adding 4 tablespoons of powdered coffee to the milk while heating it.

ESTHER'S RASPBERRY TORTONI SURPRISE

Biscuit tortoni and raspberry sherbert are both excellent desserts by themselves, but when combined they make an absolutely superb ending for a meal.

A layer of raspberry sherbert, at least an inch thick, then a layer of biscuit tortoni, at least 1½ inches thick, molded in a spring form pan or in any fancy mold of your choice. A heart-shape mold filled with this combination makes a perfect dessert for Valentine's day. Even the colors are right. Keep the mold in the freezing compartment of the refrigerator or in the deep freeze until serving time, unmold onto an attractive serving dish, and serve as is or garnish to suit your desires and taste. If using a spring form, put the layer of raspberry sherbert first; if using a regular mold, put the biscuit tortoni first, for when serving, the raspberry sherbert should be on the bottom.

Raspberry sherbert from a good ice cream company is usually just as good as any made in the home and is more convenient as well as less expensive. To serve 6 to 8 people you will need 1 quart of sherbert.

BISCUIT TORTONI

2 *teaspoons gelatin*	6 *tablespoons sherry or*
¼ *cup cold water*	*Madeira*
1⅓ *cups light corn syrup*	1 *cup macaroons, crumbled*
4 *egg yolks*	½ *cup almonds, chopped*
½ *teaspoon salt*	*coarsely*

2 *cups heavy cream, whipped*

Soften the gelatin in the cold water. Heat the corn syrup and stir in the softened gelatin; stir over low heat until gelatin is completely dissolved. Beat the egg yolks until light and gradually stir them into the syrup mixture. Cool to room temperature. Add the salt and sherry. If the macaroons are moist, toast them a bit before crumbling them into the mixture. Add ¼ cup of the almonds, use the remaining ¼ cup to sprinkle on top before serving. Fold in the whipped cream. Spread this mixture over the top of the sherbert in a spring mold form. If using a mold, put the mixture into the mold and put into the freezer compartment of the refrigerator for an hour before unmolding to serve. It may, of course, be made well in advance and held in the freezer indefinitely.

FROZEN RASPBERRY AND PEACH MOUSSE

1½ cups raspberries, mashed
    lightly
¾ cup peaches, mashed
    lightly

1 cup sugar
1½ cups heavy cream,
    whipped

Combine the raspberries, peaches, and sugar. Mix well and then fold in the whipped cream. Turn the mixture into a mold and freeze for 4 hours or until firm. This is better if not frozen too long. Loosen from mold by dipping quickly in hot water. Turn out onto a serving plate and return to freezer for 10 minutes or until ready to serve. Garnish with fresh whole raspberries and sliced peaches.

Fruit Desserts

FRESH FRUIT is a safe and sane way to end a meal; in fact, some meals demand a fruit ending. But good as fresh fruit is, it isn't going to be a fitting climax for a meal designed to prove your cooking know-how. A little tampering with the fruit will make it memorable to the diners. Recipes will make six servings.

PEARS HÉLÈNE

The pear is a succulent fruit that lends itself to many more uses than it is generally given credit for. It is too much restricted to eating out of hand or to being served in its natural state with cheese. Poach the pear in a vanilla or wine syrup and you have the basis for many an exciting dessert. The best variety of pear for desserts is the Bartlett, a "pear-shaped" pear with a clear yellow skin. Bartlett pears are the most abundant and the cheapest in the fall, but they are in the market all year round.

6 *fresh pears, ripe but firm*
¾ *cup sugar*
1½ *cups water*
1 *two-inch piece of vanilla bean or 1 teaspoon vanilla extract*

Vanilla ice cream
Chocolate sauce, heated or cold, to suit your taste

Peel the pears and cut in half lengthwise. Remove cores. Combine the sugar, water, and vanilla in a saucepan and bring to the boil. Add 3 or 4 pear-halves at a time, as many as can comfortably fit into the pan and be covered with the syrup, and cook gently until just tender. Do not overcook; the pears must retain their shape and firmness. Chill the poached pears in the syrup.

When ready to serve put a scoop or ball of vanilla ice cream into each dessert or sherbert dish, arrange 2 pear-halves on the ice cream and mask the whole with chocolate sauce.

PEARS FLAMBÉ

6 *fresh pears*
¾ *cup sugar*
1½ *cups water*
1 *inch piece of vanilla bean or* ¾ *teaspoon vanilla extract*

1 *cup apricot preserves*
2 *tablespoons cornstarch dissolved in* ¼ *cup water*
½ *cup rum*

Peel and core the pears and cut in half lengthwise. Combine the sugar, water, and vanilla in a saucepan and bring to a boil, stirring. Add 3 or 4 pear-halves at a time and poach gently until just tender. After the pears are cooked, continue to cook the syrup until it is reduced to about 1 cup. Add the apricot preserves and bring to a boil, then slowly stir in the cornstarch that has been dissolved in ¼ cup cold water. Cook, stirring, until sauce is thickened. If sauce is not thick enough to coat the pears, add a bit of additional cornstarch. Pour the sauce over the pears and keep warm. When ready to serve, heat the rum. Pour over the pears at the table and ignite immediately. The pears may be poached well in advance and the sauce made, and both can be reheated just before serving. Or reheat just the sauce and serve the pears cold. Either way is delicious.

PEARS WITH ZABAGLIONE SAUCE

Here are hot pears with cold sauce or cold pears with hot sauce, as the mood strikes you. These are two desserts from one recipe, really, for the contrast between cold pears and hot sauce or vice versa makes for a big difference in flavor and texture.

> 6 fresh pears, poached as directed in
>   Pears Hélène (see recipe)
> Zabaglione Sauce (see recipe)

Arrange 2 poached pear-halves in each dessert dish and cover with the sauce.

PEAR DELIGHT

6 pears   ½ cup water
¾ cup sugar   1 tablespoon lemon juice
3 tablespoons apricot jam   Pastry Cream I (see recipe)
          ¼ cup cognac or rum

Peel and core the pears and cut in half lengthwise. Combine in a saucepan the sugar, apricot jam, water, and lemon juice, and bring to a boil. Put in 3 or 4 pear-halves at a time and poach until just tender, about 6 or 7 minutes. Stir in rum or cognac. Chill the pears in the syrup. Make Pastry Cream. Arrange the pear-halves on a serving dish, saving the syrup, and mound the Pastry Cream on top with a spoon, or pipe it on with a pastry bag. Pour the syrup over all and serve.

PEARS IN WINE

6 *fresh pears*
1 *cup sugar*
½ *cup red wine*

1 *2-inch piece of stick cinamon*
1 *small piece lemon peel*

¼ *cup cognac or rum, heated*

Peel and core pears and cut in half lengthwise. In a saucepan combine the sugar, wine, cinnamon, and lemon peel. Bring to a boil, stirring. Add 3 or 4 pear-halves at a time and cook gently until just tender. Simmer the syrup until it has reduced to ½ its original quantity. Arrange the pears in a serving dish and pour the syrup over the pears and chill. At the table pour the cognac or rum over the pears and ignite. When flame dies down, dish out the individual portions.

PÊCHE ITALIENNE

Beautiful and delicious.

6 *fresh peaches*
1 *cup sugar*
⅔ *cup water*
2-inch piece vanilla bean or
  2 *teaspoons vanilla extract*
1 *cup Pastry Cream I (see recipe)*

½ *to 1 cup crumbled macaroons*
12 *small thin rounds of sponge cake*
Whipped cream for garnish

Peel, cut in half, and stone the peaches. Combine the sugar, water, and vanilla, and bring to a boil. Add the peach halves to the mixture 3 or 4 at a time, and poach until just tender. Cool them in the syrup and then chill in the refrigerator.

Make Pastry Cream. Stir in the crumbled macaroons until the cream will hold no more. Arrange peach halves on a serving plate. Place a round of sponge cake on each peach, then mound the Pastry Cream mixture on top and garnish each with whipped cream.

Pies and Tarts

AMERICANS LOVE PIES and they should, for pies make mighty fine eating. Most housewives have a large repertoire of pies, so given here are just a few that do not appear in the usual list of flavors. Tarts are made with a rich short-crust pastry, a pleasant change from pie-crust pastry, but not a substitute for it. Short Crust pastry (see p. 151) and Pie Crust pastry (see p. 91) each has its own merits and own uses.

Tart pastry, like pie crust, may be filled with fruit or other fillings and then baked, or it may be baked "blind," that is, the crust is thoroughly baked and then filled with a separately prepared mixture. To bake blind, line the pastry with a good-sized piece of oiled paper or tin foil weighted down with pebbles or beans. This prevents the pastry from shrinking and bulging up from the bottom of the pan. Bake for 10 minutes, then remove the paper and weights and continue to bake until golden.

These recipes yield servings for six.

BLUEBERRY CREAM TART

This tart is destined to make your reputation as a cook. It is so pretty and so delicious that the most discriminate of gourmets will applaud, but it is not so esoteric that it will intimidate those lovers of "good plain fare."

Raspberries, blackberries, or any other of your favorite berries may be substituted for the blueberries in this recipe.

SHORT CRUST

This makes sufficient pastry for 6 tart shells or one 8-inch shell.

1½ to 2 cups flour	1 egg yolk
⅛ teaspoon salt	1½ to 2 tablespoons cold
6 ounces (¾ stick) butter	water (lemon juice may
or margarine	be substituted for 1
1 tablespoon sugar	tablespoon water)

Sift the flour with the salt into a mixing bowl. Cut in the butter or margarine and blend it with pastry blender, with your fingers, or with two knives until the mixture resembles fine bread crumbs. Add the egg yolk and water and mix to a firm dough. Knead lightly on a floured board for 3 minutes. Chill the pastry for 15 minutes before using for easier handling. If the pastry has been kept in the refrigerator for some time it will be brittle and should be allowed to stand at room temperature until malleable. Roll out the pastry on a lightly floured board or pastry cloth to ¼-inch thickness, line tart shells or an 8-inch flan ring or shell. Bake at 375° for 20 minutes or until golden and done. If made ahead of time, the shells can be reheated before filling.

Spread a Crème Anglaise (see recipe) evenly in the shell to a depth of about one inch, then cover completely with Blueberry Topping (recipe below), and garnish with whipped cream. Pipe the whipped cream through a pastry tube into rosettes all around the edge of the tart. If you do not have a pastry tube, make an edging of whipped cream with a spoon and your finger. It is much more attractive to have the whipped cream making a border, leaving the glossy fruit to show, than to cover the whole with it.

Blueberry Topping

2 cups blueberries
2 tablespoons water
1 tablespoon lemon juice
⅓ cup sugar (or more to suit taste)

4 teaspoons cornstarch dissolved in cold water

Place berries, water, lemon juice, and sugar in a pan and bring slowly to a boil. When sugar is completely dissolved and berries just beginning to soften, gradually stir in the cornstarch. You may not need all the cornstarch so stop when the desired consistency is reached. Cook until thick enough to spread. Cool.

MACAROON TARTLETS

Short-Crust pastry (see recipe)
Raspberry jam (1 teaspoon of jam for each tartlet)

2 egg whites
½ cup sugar
5 ounces ground almonds

Prepare pastry, roll out fairly thinly and line the patty pans or tart pans. Cut the trimmings into thin strips for the decoration. Put a teaspoon of jam on the bottom of each tart. Beat the egg white until peaks are just beginning to form, add the sugar a little at a time and continue to beat until the mixture stands in firm glossy peaks. Fold in the ground almonds. Divide the mixture among the prepared tins. This is sufficient for 6 3-inch tarts or 12 1½ to 2-inch tarts. Decorate the top of each with a cross made from the strips of pastry and bake at 350° for 25 minutes. Serve at room temperature.

FRESH PEACH TART

1 *baked 9-inch pie or tart*   *Fresh peaches, sliced*
  shell (see recipe)   *Whipped cream for garnish*
1 *recipe Pastry Cream 1*
  (see recipe)

Cover the baked Pie Crust (see recipe) or tart shell
with the Pastry Cream. Peel sliced peaches, dip into lemon
and water solution or water and ascorbic solution to keep
peaches from discoloring. Then sugar slices to taste and
allow to stand for at least 10 minutes. Now arrange the
slices in neat concentric circles on top of the Pastry Cream.
Garnish with whipped cream that has been sweetened to
taste and flavored with vanilla. Keep in the refrigerator
until serving.

Fresh strawberries, raspberries, or blueberries may be
substituted for the peaches. When using blueberries, however, you will want to cook some of them with sugar and
a bit of flour to make a glaze, for fresh blueberries do not
soak up sugar. Put a layer of fresh blueberries on the
Pastry Cream, then spread the cooked sweetened berries
on top.

OPEN-FACE APPLE PIE

This is a very nice variation on that old favorite, apple
pie, and one that has a great deal of eye appeal.

1 *9-inch pie shell*   3 *tablespoons cinnamon*
8 *medium-sized tart apples*   1 *tablespoon flour*
1 *cup sugar*   4 *tablespoons butter, melted*

Make a pie shell according to recipe for Pie Crust. Bake
for 5 to 6 minutes or just long enough to give a slight

glaze to the surface. This prevents the fruit juices from soaking in and making the crust soggy. Peel the apples, cut into quarters, and remove core. Place the apple quarters into a colander and put the colander over a pan of boiling water and permit them to steam until they are just beginning to get a slightly transparent appearance. If you use an early green transparent apple or a wealthy, you may omit the steaming as these are fast-cooking apples. Combine the sugar, cinnamon, and flour, and roll each apple quarter in this mixture, arranging the quarters overlapping in neat concentric circles in the pie shell. If there is any sugar mixture remaining, sprinkle it over the top. Drip the melted butter over the top and bake for ½ hour at 375° or until the apples are tender and gooey-looking. You want the apples to retain their shape or the pie will not be attractive. Serve the pie at room temperature or chilled, topped with whipped cream that you have sweetened to taste with sugar and flavored wih vanilla.

SOUR CREAM APPLE PIE

Follow directions for Open-Face Apple Pie in preceding recipe, substituting 1 cup of sour cream for the melted butter. Spread the sour cream over the top of the neatly arranged apples and bake as directed. Serve chilled.

SOUR CREAM PEACH PIE

Substitute peaches for apples in preceding recipe. It is not necessary to steam the peaches.

AND SOMETHING IN-BETWEEN

This book was originally intended as a collection of recipes for first courses and desserts, but I couldn't resist adding a few recipes and suggestions for the course that comes in between, all those recipes and ideas that have collected in my kitchen notebook since I wrote my last cookbook, *Gourmet Kitchen,* and recipes that I have regretted not having had in time to be included in that book.

Beef

FILET MIGNON AUX FINES HERBES

I am in sympathy with those who feel that a good steak shouldn't be tampered with—just broil, season, and serve. However, every now and then it is exciting and palate-exhilarating to gild the steak. This recipe by no means kills that wonderful beef taste; rather, it points it up, accentuates the excellence of the meat.

1 tablespoon each, chopped:
  parsley
  chives
  basil
  thyme or rosemary
	Filet mignon 1 inch thick for
	  six persons
	6 tablespoons butter
	1 cup white wine
	Salt and pepper to taste

Mix the finely chopped herbs and sprinkle on the steaks. Put in the refrigerator for at least 8 hours or overnight. Remove from refrigerator and let herbed steaks stand at room temperature for 2 hours before cooking. Put the butter in a large skillet over high heat. When butter begins to sizzle, put in the steaks and cook quickly until the desired degree of doneness. Steak is, of course, always tastier if cooked rare—about 3 minutes on each side. Remove from pan to serving platter. Pour the wine into the pan and swirl it around until it has picked up all the nice brown butter and the herbs that have fallen from the steaks. Salt and pepper the steaks and then pour over the wine sauce. Serve immediately.

STEAK AU POIVRE

This is a dish to remember. It is not one you may want to eat often, but every now and then it is a real taste treat. There are several versions of this dish, but I think this one with a simple sauce is the best, for it permits the quality of the steak to come through.

6 *tablespoons* *peppercorns,*
coarsely crushed in a mor-
tar or on a board with a
hammer
6 *1-inch-thick tenderloin*
steaks, or a 1 inch sirloin
cut into 6 servings

2 *tablespoons butter*
2 *tablespoons oil*
1 *cup white wine*
2 *tablespoons brandy*
2 *tablespoons butter*

Pound the coarsely ground peppercorns firmly into both sides of the steak with a potato masher or a hammer. In a large skillet, melt the butter and oil over a high flame. When it begins to sizzle, put in the steak and cook quickly until the desired degree of doneness. It will be tastier and more tender if cooked rare. Remove the steaks to a serving platter. Stir the wine and brandy into the pan juices. Simmer on a low flame for 2 minutes, add 2 tablespoons of butter and pour it, loose pepper and all, over the steak. Serve immediately.

ENTRECÔTE MARCHAND AU VIN

A ½- to 1-inch-thick sirloin or rib steak is good for this. This is rather a strong sauce and ideal if you are in doubt as to the quality or flavor of the beef.

2 tablespoons finely chopped onion	2 tablespoons tomato purée
12 tablespoons butter	2 tablespoons Madeira or sherry
Teaspoon flour	Steak for 6 persons
2 cups red wine	
3 cloves garlic, crushed or mashed	

Cook the finely chopped onion in the butter until it is tender but not brown. Sprinkle with the flour and blend. Add the wine and bring to a slow boil. Then add the garlic, tomato purée, and Madeira. Lower flame and simmer for ½ hour.

Broil the steak at high heat so that it will brown quickly and still remain juicy and pink inside. Cut into serving pieces, arrange on a platter, and pour the sauce over all.

SWISS STEAK

I am not certain that "Swiss Steak" properly describes this very tasty steak dish. It resembles other Swiss Steak I have eaten only in that it is round steak cooked for a long time in a sauce. This sauce is thick and luscious, smelling and tasting of a variety of subtle seasonings.

⅔ cup flour	2 pounds round steak, cut 1 inch thick
⅔ teaspoon salt	1 teaspoon marjoram
⅓ teaspoon pepper	½ teaspoon oregano
⅛ teaspoon cayenne	1 large clove garlic, minced
Butter or suet for sautéing	1 cup boiling water
2 onions, sliced thinly	⅔ cup white wine

Cut the steak into serving pieces. Mix the flour, salt, pepper, and cayenne and pound and rub it into the steak. This is rather a laborious process, but a very important one, so don't give up. All the flour must be absorbed by the steak. This gives the meat its tenderness and the sauce its lovely thick quality. Pound in as much of the flour as you can, then let the steak stand for 15 to 30 minutes and pound and rub in some more. Do this until all the flour has been used. Put a generous amount of butter or suet into a heavy skillet and brown the onions and the steak. Sprinkle the herbs and minced garlic onto the steak. Mix the boiling water and white wine and pour it into the skillet, being careful not to wash the herbs off the steak. Cover very tightly and simmer on a low, low flame for 1½ to 2 hours, or until the meat is very tender and the sauce thick. Baste the meat frequently. If sauce should reduce too much during the cooking, add more water and wine. This is excellent served with baked Idaho potatoes.

FILET DE BOEUF BORGERHOFF

That good beef should not be tampered with is true, but any recipe that points up the goodness of high quality filet of beef is to be cherished. This method of presenting a filet does just that. It makes a good steak even better without killing any of the beefiness.

Butter for sautéing	*Salt and pepper to taste*
6 rounds of French bread,	*⅓ cup warmed brandy*
cut ¾ inch thick	*½ cup Madeira*
6 filets of beef, cut an inch	*3 tablespoons chopped parsley*
thick	

Heat a generous amount of butter in a heavy skillet, sauté the rounds of French bread until golden and crisp on the edges. Remove the bread and keep it warm. Add more butter to the pan and sauté the steaks for 2½ minutes on each side, or longer if you want them more than medium rare. Place a filet on each round of bread, season with salt and pepper, pour over the warm brandy and set it aflame. Pour the Madeira into the pan in which the steak was cooked and swirl around. When the flame dies out on the steaks, pour the juices from the pan over them and sprinkle with chopped parsley. Serve piping hot.

SIRLOIN WITH WHITE WINE SAUCE

Here's that thick juicy sirloin grilled or broiled and given an extra fillip by the mere pouring on of a simple white wine sauce.

3 *minced shallots*	¾ *cup dry white wine*
2 *tablespoons butter*	2 *teaspoons minced parsley*
1 *tablespoon mild prepared mustard of a good grade*	*Salt and pepper*
	1½ *inch thick sirloin for 6*

Sauté the minced shallots in the butter over a low flame until soft. Add the prepared mustard and wine, simmer for 1 minute, add the parsley, salt, and pepper, and simmer for 2 more minutes.

Broil the steak, put on a serving platter, and slice in thin slices across the grain, as for London broil. Pour the sauce over the steak slices and serve immediately.

BEEF EN BROCHETTE WITH BOURBON OR COGNAC

There is always a festive feeling about meat on skewers, whether the skewers are long or short. The skewers used for this dish must of necessity be short since they must fit into a pan after the meat has been broiled or grilled.

½ cup olive oil
¼ cup wine vinegar
¼ teaspoon pepper
1 teaspoon salt
1 teaspoon bitters
¼ cup bourbon or cognac

1 large clove garlic, crushed
1½ pounds sirloin, cut into 1½-inch cubes
4 firm tomatoes
4 medium onions, peeled

Combine the oil, vinegar, pepper, salt, bitters, and crushed garlic. Put the beef cubes into this marinade and let stand for 2 hours. Cut the tomatoes and onions into large chunks and thread on skewers alternately with the beef. Cook under a hot broiler or on a grill until brown on the outside but still juicy and pink inside, about 4 minutes on each side. Heat the bourbon or cognac in a large skillet or chafing dish. Place the skewers in the pan and ignite the bourbon or cognac. When the flame dies out, serve immediately, and spoon the juices in the pan over the skewers.

STEAK TERIYAKI

⅓ cup soy sauce
⅔ cup cold water
1 piece whole ginger that has been soaked in water until soft
2 cloves garlic, crushed
2 teaspoons sugar

1 tablespoon vinegar
½ teaspoon salt
¼ teaspoon pepper
1½ pounds round steak
2 teaspoons cornstarch dissolved in cold water

Combine the soy sauce, water, ginger, garlic, sugar, vinegar, salt, and pepper. Marinade the steak in this sauce for at least 8 hours. When ready to eat, fry steak in butter until the desired degree of doneness. Heat the marinade and thicken with the cornstarch dissolved in water. Simmer for 5 minutes. Serve with boiled rice.

Lamb

ARMENIAN SHISH KEBAB

Shish Kebab is a favorite in all the Middle Eastern countries, all variations of it more or less alike, yet all a bit different. This Armenian version is the most distinctive, employing sour cream in the marinade instead of wine and oil.

4 *cloves of garlic, crushed or chopped fine*
1½ *teaspoons salt*
½ *teaspoon ginger*
½ *teaspoon allspice*
½ *teaspoon cloves*

½ *teaspoon chopped bay leaves*
½ *teaspoon paprika*
½ *teaspoon pepper*
Leg of spring lamb, cut into 1-inch cubes

1 *pint sour cream*

Mix all the spices together in a large bowl. Wash the meat and roll the cubes in the spices. Pour the sour cream over it, cover tightly, and store in the refrigerator for 3 days. When ready to cook, put on skewers with hunks of tomato, slices of green pepper, and, if you like, onion rings. Broil until brown on all sides but still slightly pink inside. Catch the drippings and spoon over the meat on the plates. Serve with rice pilaf and a green salad.

Veal

VEAL AU MADEIRA

Sad but true that Madeira is an expensive wine in this country. However, a little Madeira does so much for so many meats that it is well worth the investment. This is the simplest of dishes to prepare but one of the most elegant to serve and eat.

*Veal scallops or tenderloin
cut thin, for 6 persons*
Salt and pepper to taste

Flour for dredging
4 tablespoons butter
¾ cup Madeira

Have the veal cut very thin. Sprinkle the meat with salt and pepper and dredge each piece lightly with flour. Melt the butter in a large skillet and when it is hot and bubbly, put in the veal and cook quickly on high heat until brown on both sides. Arrange the veal slices on a serving platter. Pour the Madeira into the pan and swirl it around over a low flame until it has picked up all the brown crust and drippings. Pour over the meat and serve immediately.

VEAL WITH TARRAGONED CREAM

This is my favorite veal dish. It is delicate and delicious.

3 *tablespoons butter*
1 *tablespoon olive oil*
2 *tablespoons minced shallots*
Salt
Tenderloin of veal for 6 persons, cut into thin round

medallions, *or cutlet of*
veal pounded thin and cut
into 2-inch square pieces
4 *tablespoons tarragon*
   vinegar
1½ *cups heavy cream*
½ *teaspoon freshly ground pepper*

Put the butter and oil into a skillet over a medium flame. When it is hot and bubbly, put in the minced shallot and cook, stirring until it is brown. Salt the medallions or pieces of veal and put them into the foaming butter and cook on both sides until brown. Remove meat to a serving platter to keep warm. Pour the tarragon vinegar into the pan, swirl it around, and then pour in the heavy cream; stir well. Let it boil vigorously for 1 minute. Stir in the freshly ground pepper. Pour sauce over the veal.

This can be made ahead of time. The meat must then be put into the sauce and reheated in the sauce. Serve with fluffy boiled rice.

VEAL CASSEROLE

This casserole is a wonderful way to make an inexpensive cut of veal delectable.

2 *pounds of trimmed veal*
   shoulder cut into cubes
   (*stewing veal may be used*)
2 *tablespoons flour*
2 *teaspoons salt*

½ *teaspoon pepper*
3 *tablespoons butter or*
   cooking oil
2 *cups chopped onions*
1 *clove garlic, minced*
1½ *cups sour cream*

Dredge the cubed veal in the flour mixed with the salt and pepper. Heat the butter or oil in a skillet and add the meat, onions, and garlic. Cook and stir until the onions and meat are nicely browned. Transfer to a casserole and stir in the sour cream. Cover and bake at 350° until the veal is tender, about 1½ to 2 hours.

VEAL PARMIGIANA

A hearty, tasty dish that is reminiscent of Italy in its appearance, smell, and taste, as well as in name. It is a bit of trouble to make but well worth the trouble if you like eggplant.

1 *medium-sized eggplant, peeled, sliced thin, and salted*
Butter and oil for frying
6 *fresh tomatoes, or equivalent amount of canned tomatoes if fresh ones are out of season*
2 *large onions, chopped fine*

1 *clove garlic, minced*
2 *pounds veal cutlet, cut into serving pieces and pounded thin*
Flour seasoned with salt and pepper
1 *pound mozzarella*
Sauce (recipe below)
⅔ *cup grated Parmesan*

Sprinkle the eggplant slices generously with salt and let stand for ½ hour. Drain well and fry in the butter and oil until translucent and tender. Drain on absorbent paper. Cut the tomatoes in thick slices and add to the pan with the chopped onion and garlic. Simmer for 5 minutes. Put the eggplant slices in the bottom of a large, rather shallow (about 2 inches) baking dish and cover with the tomato mixture. Now dredge the veal lightly in flour that you have seasoned with salt and pepper. Add butter to the pan and sauté the veal until brown on both sides. Arrange the veal slices on top of the vegetables. Cover the veal with slices of mozzarella.

Pour the sauce over the dish and then sprinkle the entire surface with the Parmesan. Bake for 30 minutes at 375°. If not sufficiently brown and bubbly on top, put under a hot broiler for a few minutes. Bring the baking dish directly to the table.

Sauce

2 tablespoons butter	1 cup chicken stock or
1 tablespoon flour	bouillon
1 tablespoon tomato paste	⅔ cup red wine

Melt the butter in a pan, blend in the flour, and then slowly stir in the tomato paste, stock, and wine. Simmer until smooth and slightly thickened.

Kidneys

KIDNEYS FLAMBÉ À LA MOUTARDE

A dish to please the most exacting palate and one that is quick and easy to prepare.

6 *veal kidneys*	*Salt and pepper*
4 *tablespoons butter*	1½ *teaspoons Dijon mustard*
½ *cup warm brandy*	1½ *cups heavy cream*

Clean and skin the kidneys; cut in half and remove all the fat and tissue. Slice the kidneys and sauté them in the butter for 2 or 3 minutes, or until just done. Overcooking toughens kidneys. Pour on the warm brandy and ignite. When flame dies out, salt and pepper the kidneys and stir the mustard into the juices in the pan. Pour in the cream and stir until blended. Heat thoroughly. Serve with fluffy boiled rice.

KIDNEYS FLAMBÉ

A dish flaming with brandy is always exciting and flavorful. This recipe goes together much like the preceding one but the end result is quite different.

6 *veal kidneys*
Bacon fat for sautéing, about
    2 tablespoons
2 *shallots, minced, or equiva-*
    lent amount of minced
    onion

1 *cup finely sliced*
    mushrooms
3 *tablespoons butter*
Salt and pepper
1 *cup heavy cream*
⅓ *cup warm brandy*

Clean the kidneys of all fat and membrane and cut into thin slices. Melt the bacon fat in a skillet and sauté the kidneys for 2 minutes. Add the shallot or onion, the mushrooms, butter, and salt and pepper. Cook, covered, for 4 minutes. Stir in the cream and bring to a boil. Pour on the brandy and set aflame. Shake the pan until the flame dies and serve the kidneys with boiled rice or on toast.

KIDNEYS WITH RED WINE

Another tasty way to present kidneys is this:

6 *veal kidneys*
Salt and pepper
4 *to 5 tablespoons butter*
1 *large onion, finely chopped*

1 *cup thinly sliced*
    mushrooms
2 *tablespoons flour*
1 *cup red wine*
½ *cup water*

Remove all fat and membrane from the kidneys and cut into bite-size pieces. Sprinkle the kidneys with salt and pepper and brown the pieces quickly in the hot butter with the onion and mushrooms, or about 4 minutes. Sprinkle the flour over the kidneys and blend well. Slowly stir in the wine and water. Let the mixture simmer for 3 minutes. Serve with rice.

Pheasant and Duck

PHEASANT AU MADEIRA AND CREAM

Pheasant is not an everyday affair, but every now and again during the pheasant season you may be presented with a bird or two by one of your shooting friends. And what to do with it? Since it is a rare bird and a delicacy, you want to make the most of it. And I assure you this recipe does make the most of any pheasant. It sounds elaborate, but it is really simpler than most simple-sounding procedures for dealing with pheasant.

Pheasant for 6 persons, cut into serving pieces
½ cup heavy cream
Flour for dredging
Salt and pepper
Butter for sautéing

1½ cups Madeira
1 cup heavy cream
2 cups seedless white grapes
12 artichoke hearts (preferably canned)

Cut up the pheasants into serving pieces. Dip each piece into heavy cream and then into flour seasoned with salt and pepper. Heat a generous amount of butter in a skillet and brown the pheasant on all sides. Place the pheasant in a casserole and pour over it the Madeira.

Cover closely and bake for 1 hour, or until tender, at 350°. Remove pheasant to a serving platter and keep it warm. Place the casserole on a low flame and stir in the cup of heavy cream. When cream is hot, add the white grapes and the artichoke hearts. If using canned hearts, rinse thoroughly to remove all traces of the brine. Do not cook after the addition of grapes and artichoke hearts. Serve with wild rice. Nothing less elegant will do for this truly makes a pheasant of rare plumage.

PHEASANT À LA CRÈME ET COGNAC

Another delightful and delicious way to serve up that bird that your hunter-husband or friend presents to you as a special treat is this.

Pheasant for 6 persons	*2 cups heavy cream*
4 strips of bacon	*3 egg yolks*
½ cup brandy	*Salt and pepper*
2 tablespoons butter	

After cleaning and plucking, cover whole birds with the strips of bacon and place in a deep casserole. Roast uncovered at 375° for ½ hour, or until the breasts are tender when pricked with a fork. Now remove from casserole and slice off all the breast meat in as large slices as you can and set aside to keep warm. Scrape and cut off all the remaining meat from the carcass and chop fine. Return the chopped meat to the casserole and simmer over low heat for 5 minutes. Skim off excess fat. Add ¼ cup of the brandy and ignite. When flame dies down, gradually stir in the cream mixed with the egg yolks and the salt and pepper. Cook and stir over low heat until sauce has thickened slightly, but do not boil. Stir in the remaining ¼ cup of brandy and the butter. Strain the sauce and pour over the breasts and serve with an accompanying bowl of wild rice.

PHEASANT (OR DUCK) À L'ORANGE

Pheasant or duck for 6
  persons
3 oranges
1 lemon

3 tablespoons vinegar
1 tablespoon sugar
3 tablespoons Cointreau,
  Grand Marnier, or brandy
½ cup hot chicken stock or consommé

Roast the pheasant or ducks in a 325° oven for 20 minutes per pound or until tender when pierced with a fork. Baste frequently. If using pheasant, rub the bird well with butter and melt additional butter for basting.

Grate coarsely the rind of 2 oranges and 1 lemon. Blanch the rind in boiling water for ½ minute and drain. Combine the vinegar and sugar in a small pan and simmer over low heat until the mixture begins to caramelize. Add the juice of the 2 oranges and 1 lemon and simmer together for 2 minutes. Add the blanched rinds. When the birds are done, remove to a serving platter and decorate with thin slices of an orange, peeled and halved. Skim all excess fat from the pan juices. There will be a great deal more with duck than with pheasant. Pour in the liqueur or brandy and the stock and scrape in all the brown glaze in the pan. Let boil up for a second and then add this juice to the orange sauce, reheat it and pour a little of it over the birds. Serve the rest in a sauceboat to be poured over each serving.

BEN'S DUCK

Duck and oranges seem to have a natural affinity. The combination is always good, and this version has the advantage of being simpler to prepare than most.

2 ducks, quartered
Salt and pepper
1 cup water
⅛ teaspoon each of thyme, marjoram, and sage
2 teaspoons cornstarch dissolved in cold water

Juice and pulp of 3 oranges
Juice of ½ lemon
1 tablespoon grated orange rind
2 teaspoons sugar

Sprinkle the ducks with salt and pepper. Place in a deep casserole with 1 cup of water, and distribute the herbs over the duck. Cover closely and bake at 300° for 2 hours. Remove duck sections to a serving platter and keep warm. Thicken the sauce with the cornstarch dissolved in water, stir in the orange juice, pulp, lemon juice, and grated orange rind and sugar. Stir over low heat until well-blended. Pour the sauce over the quarters of duck and serve.

DUCK ON A SPIT WITH APRICOT GLAZE

Duck for 6 persons
Salt and pepper
1 teaspoon powdered ginger for each duck

1 cup apricot jam mixed with
½ cup apricot juice or orange juice

Wipe the ducks with a damp cloth. Sprinkle the inside and outside of ducks with salt and pepper and rub a teaspoon of ginger on the outside of each duck to be cooked. Place the ducks on a spit above a medium fire, and, after basting with the mixture of jam and juice, start the rotating. If the fire is kept at a moderate heat and the ducks are about 6 inches from the flames, they should be allowed to rotate for 3 hours, basting them every ½ hour for the first 2 hours, and then basting them every 10 to 15 minutes for the last hour. If at the end of this time they are still not very tender, lower spit and cook them for another ½ hour or until very well-done. They should be beautifully brown and glazed.

If you desire a sauce, take another cup of apricot jam, dilute it with ½ cup of juice, either apricot or orange, heat, and serve in a sauce boat.

This duck and apricot combination is so very good that you may want to have it when it isn't convenient to use an open fire and spit or a rotisserie. Put an apple or an onion inside each duck and then place the duck in a roasting pan in a 350° oven. After an hour, start basting the ducks with the apricot jam and juice mixture. Baste every 10 minutes for an hour. If duck is still not brown and very well-done, continue to bake and baste until it is.

Rock Cornish Hen

ROCK CORNISH HEN WITH BLACK CHERRIES
(Duck may be treated in same way)

6 *small Cornish hens or 3* *Salt and pepper*
  large ones split 6 *tablespoons butter*

Salt and pepper the hens. Rub a generous amount of butter on each, and place in a roasting pan and roast at 350° for 1 to 1½ hours or until very tender, basting from time to time with drippings and additional melted butter.

BLACK CHERRY SAUCE

2 *cups port*
2 *whole cloves*
1/16 *teaspoon each of nut-meg, allspice, and thyme*
1 *teaspoon grated orange rind*
Drippings from the roasting pan, rinsed loose with ½
cup Chicken Stock or bouillon
½ *cup red currant jelly*
1 *cup black cherries*
Juice of 1 orange
2 *tablespoons sweet butter*
2 *teaspoons cornstarch dis-solved in water*

Combine the port, spices, and grated rind, and simmer until reduced to half the quantity. After the hens have been removed from the roasting pan, pour in ½ cup of stock and stir it around until all the good brown glaze has been picked up. Then pour this juice into the pan with the port. Stir in the currant jelly. When it has dissolved, add the black cherries, orange juice, and butter. Bring to a boil and gradually stir in the dissolved cornstarch. Do this bit by bit, stopping when you have reached the consistency you like. Pour some of the sauce over the hens and serve the remainder in a sauceboat. This dish really deserves wild rice, but if your budget is a bit strained, white rice would make a fine substitute.

Chicken

CHICKEN WITH AROMATIC SAUCE

A delicious way to serve chicken. It is simple to prepare and has the added advantage of being even better if prepared ahead of time and reheated in the sauce.

2 2- to 3-pound chickens cut into serving pieces
Salt and pepper
½ cup butter
⅓ cup brandy, warmed
6 shallots, finely chopped, or

1 small onion, finely chopped
1 tablespoon chopped parsley
¼ teaspoon thyme
⅔ cup dry white wine
⅔ cup heavy cream

Season the chicken pieces with salt and pepper. Heat the butter in a large skillet and brown the chicken on all sides. Lower the heat, cover the chicken and cook for 12 minutes. Pour on the warmed brandy and ignite. Shake the pan until the flame dies out. Add the shallot or onion, the parsley, thyme, and wine. Blend the sauce well, cover, and continue to cook 20 minutes longer or until the chicken is tender. Stir in the heavy cream. Allow to heat thoroughly, but do not boil. Arrange the chicken on a platter and pour the sauce over it.

CHICKEN IN PARMESAN CREAM SAUCE

2 2- to 3-pound frying chickens, cut into serving pieces
Salt and pepper
6 tablespoons butter
2 tablespoons flour

1 cup light cream
⅔ cup grated Parmesan
  cheese
3 egg yolks, beaten
½ cup fresh bread crumbs

Season chicken with salt and pepper. Melt 4 tablespoons of the butter in a skillet and sauté the chicken
pieces until golden on all sides. Cover skillet closely and
cook on low heat for about ½ hour, or until chicken is
tender. In a saucepan melt the remaining 2 tablespoons
butter and blend in the flour. Stir in the cream, and when
thickened and smooth, remove from the fire and stir in 2
tablespoons cheese. After warming the beaten egg yolks
with a bit of the sauce, stir them carefully into the sauce.
Now sprinkle the bottom of a shallow casserole or baking
dish with ⅓ cup of the Parmesan, place the chicken pieces
on the cheese, and spoon the sauce over it and bake in a
350° oven for 20 minutes. Combine the remaining Parmesan cheese with the bread crumbs and sprinkle evenly on
top of the casserole. Place under a hot broiler until golden.

CHICKEN WITH HEARTS OF ARTICHOKE

This is a hearty meal in a dish, easy to make in a large
quantity for a buffet supper, and better if made ahead of
time and reheated.

2 2- to 3-pound chickens, cut into serving pieces
Salt and pepper
¼ cup olive oil
1 green pepper, seeded and chopped fine
2 medium onions, chopped fine
1½ cups uncooked rice
2 cups chicken broth or bouillon
1 pound cooked shrimps
2 small cans hearts of artichokes (2 hearts for each serving)
2 tomatoes peeled and chopped (if out of season, use canned tomatoes)

Season the chicken with salt and pepper and sauté in the oil with the green pepper and onion until golden. Add the uncooked rice and chicken broth. Cover and cook on low heat for 20 minutes or until rice is almost done. Transfer to a deep casserole, add the shrimps, artichokes which you have washed free of brine, tomatoes, and additional salt and pepper if needed. Cover and bake at 350° for 1 hour. Check once or twice during the baking time and if rice is becoming dry, add more chicken broth.

GRILLED HERB CHICKEN

Food cooked outside on a grill always tastes wonderful and is fun to cook as well as to eat. This chicken has not only the benefit of fresh air and a grill but also of herbs and a tasty marinade.

3 broiler chickens, cut in half
½ cup butter
2 tablespoons minced parsley
¼ teaspoon tarragon
½ teaspoon marjoram
1 cup dry white wine
½ cup salad oil
1 large clove garlic, crushed
⅓ cup soy sauce
¼ teaspoon salt

Combine the butter, parsley, tarragon, and marjoram. With a dull knife, lift the skin on the breast and legs of the chicken and spread the butter mixture under the skin.

Combine the remaining ingredients and pour over the chicken. Let stand overnight in the refrigerator. Grill the chicken halves over glowing charcoal, turning from time to time and basting frequently with the marinade. Cook until very tender, about 40 minutes.

CHICKEN BREASTS WITH CREAM

This simple but elegant dish rewards the loving care and effort expended in its preparation.

*Chicken breasts for 6 persons,
either 3 very large, or 6
small breasts, boned and
halved
Salt and pepper*

*Flour for dredging
½ to ¾ cup of butter
3 tablespoons sherry
1½ cups heavy cream*

Place the boned and halved chicken breasts between layers of waxed paper and pound until they are very thin, that is, about ¼ inch. Season the breasts with salt and pepper and dredge lightly with flour. Melt the butter in a skillet, and when it is bubbly, put in the breasts and sauté gently until golden brown on both sides. Since the breasts are thin, they will be cooked through by the time they are brown. Do not overcook or they will become dry. Pour the sherry over the breasts and then remove the breasts from the pan to a serving platter. Pour the heavy cream into the skillet and swirl around until it has picked up all the good brown glaze and juices and has thickened. The sauce should be fairly thick. Now carefully spoon the sauce onto the breasts. It should stay on top of the breasts and not run off onto the platter.

CHICKEN WITH MUSTARD

When I first ate this chicken dish the chickens were roasted on a spit, but if a spit is unavailable or inconvenient, roasting in the oven will give you, if not quite the same flavor, then an excellent dish, provided, of course, that you like the flavor of mustard.

2 *small frying chickens*
Salt and pepper
Butter
Mild prepared mustard
  (*preferably Dijon*)

2 *cups heavy cream*
Rind of 1 lemon cut into
  strips and blanched for ½
  minute in boiling water and
  drained

Season the chickens with salt and pepper and spread them all over with soft butter and prepared mustard. If roasting on a spit, be certain to have a pan underneath to collect all the juices. If using the oven, roast at 350° for 1 hour, or until tender, basting frequently with juices in pan.

Combine the heavy cream and blanched lemon rind in a saucepan and simmer over low heat for 10 minutes. When chicken is done, cut into serving pieces, skim excess fat from pan, return chicken to the pan, add the cream, place on a low heat and simmer for 3 minutes. Add more salt and pepper if necessary, and also more mustard if sauce is not sufficiently flavored.

Pork

PORK CHOPS FLAMBÉ

This is my favorite way to eat pork chops. The sauce is tangy but not overwhelming. It accentuates the goodness of the meat.

6 *large thick pork chops*
2 *teaspoons salt*
1 *teaspoon dry mustard*
½ *teaspoon black pepper*

3 *tablespoons butter*
1 *large onion, chopped*
2 *teaspoons tomato paste*
1 *cup dry white wine*

⅓ *cup brandy, warmed*

Combine the salt, mustard, and pepper and rub well into both sides of the chops. Melt 1 tablespoon of butter in a large skillet and brown the chops on both sides. Remove the chops from the pan, put in 2 tablespoons butter and sauté the onion until golden. Stir in the tomato paste and white wine. Return the chops to the pan, cover and simmer on low heat for 45 minutes or until well-done. Pour over them the warm brandy and ignite. When flame dies down, arrange the chops on a serving platter, pour over the sauce, and serve.

BAKED PORK CHOPS

6 *large pork chops*
1 *teaspoon each ground all-spice, cinnamon, marjoram, salt and pepper*
½ *teaspoon ground cloves*
½ *cup Madeira*

2 *tablespoons water*
1 *tablespoon tarragon vinegar*
3 *apples, chopped coarsely*
2 *onions, chopped coarsely*

Rub the pork chops with a mixture of the seasoning and spices. Brown quickly in a skillet and then transfer to a casserole. Combine ¼ cup of the Madeira, the water, and vinegar. Rinse out the pan the chops were browned in and pour the liquid over the chops in the casserole. Cover and roast at 400° for 20 minutes. Add to the casserole the apples and onions and continue to roast, covered at 350° for an hour, or until the chops are well done and tender. Remove the chops to a serving platter. Skim off the excess fat and stir in the remaining ¼ cup of Madeira. Now rub the sauce through a sieve and pour over the chops.

INDEX